THROUGH THE VALLEY

ONE FAMILY'S JOURNEY THROUGH PTSD

TINA SUMMERS
ANDREW SUMMERS

Inspired
Creative
Press

To the God who saved us
and
our family and friends

"... but those who hope in the Lord
will renew their strength.
They will soar on wings like eagles;
they will run and not grow weary,
they will walk and not be faint."

— ISAIAH 40:31 - HOLY BIBLE, NIV

This is a fictional retelling of true life events. To protect individual identities, some names and relationships have been changed. Remember, there are no antagonists in life. Each person depicted is the hero of their own story and the people in this story have been represented through personal experience, not necessarily as they would see themselves.

Real names have been used with permission.

Poetic license is used in some scenes.

If this story triggers any mental health concerns, please see a mental health professional.

All profits from the purchase of this book will go towards PTSD Resurrected, a non-profit that supports the recovery of those suffering from PTSD.

PROLOGUE

The call came in earlier. Tonight. 7pm.

Andy's wife nodded at him. This was it. They'd been trying all afternoon to set this up, but not now, not today.

He wasn't ready to confront his biggest fear.

The half-smile on Tina's compassionate face did him in. Letting her down made his throat tighten.

She reached out her hand, clasping his and reassuring him. "I know this is going to be hard for you, but you can do it. God is with you. Remember, you felt that this is what He wanted you to do, to ask forgiveness. Let's call Brian, he said he would go with you."

"And Jase. I want Jase there too," Andy blurted.

His heart pounded. What did he just agree to?

"Alright." Her voice was calm and soothing as if speaking to a frightened horse. "I'll call Brian and you call Jase. What time do you need to leave?"

The mental calculations briefly distracted his mind. "Tell Brian I'll pick him up at half-past three."

Five hours later, the lines of cars in front of Andy sent his anxiety skyrocketing. "We have to go back," he said, turning to Brian and Jason. He gripped the steering wheel tighter with one hand and ran the other over his shaved head. His fingers trembled as he fisted the steering wheel again.

"No, it's okay," Brian and Jason both attempted to reassure him.

It wasn't okay. His enemies were all around. Confined in grid-locked traffic. They were sitting ducks.

Brian and Jason said something else, but the words dissipated. The roaring in his ears made focusing on the road difficult. His chest had a vice around it and he struggled for breath. He was trapped, stuck in peak hour traffic going to a large Mosque in Sydney. *I don't want to do this.*

It was like trying to commit suicide all over again.

1

Middle East, Australian & Coalition Base

August, 2008

The ramp descended exposing the precious cargo within the plane. There were six Canadian soldiers this time, the caskets draped with the red and white Canadian flag. Andy's throat tightened. Not now. He had to keep it together. Inhaling sharply, he buried the emotion deep. He'd deal with it later.

"Piper, sound the call," The commanding officer yelled.

Andy's spine straightened further. He filled the bag under his arm and hit it with his hand. The sound of the drones on his bagpipes filled the open air.

"Parade, general salute. Present arms." The loud instrument almost drowned out the command.

A corridor of five hundred personnel faced inwards on either side of the procession, Canadian on one side and a coalition of Australian, New Zealand, South African and British military on the other. Commanders saluted at the front. The tarmac lights brightened the deep darkness of the night, cocooning them in a bubble.

Andy stood at attention, playing 'Flowers of the Forest' as the first casket was carried down the ramp. His fingers played the tune he heard even in his sleep. The temptation to play a different one barely even registered, he didn't want to confuse the members slow marching with the caskets.

The anguish of the pallbearers twisted their features as they struggled to keep their tears at bay. The sight gutted Andy as they passed him, but he stayed focused. He filled his lungs, blew into the mouthpiece, and squeezed the bag to carry the tune his fingers played with little thought as the procession passed him. The emotional weight for the pallbearers was far greater than the physical. They were the friends and co-workers of the fallen. He knew because he'd spent time getting to know them.

Andy's bagpipe instructor had taught him to play with emotion. Music was a powerful tool, and in this case, it would help the mates mourn their loss. Andy had spent time getting to know the fallen soldiers, so it seemed like he, himself, was grieving for a mate he'd never met.

Of the six, he thought of the two dads who wouldn't go home to their wives and children. Their friends described one as a joker, always pranking his mates, the other loved hiking and fishing. In their mid-forties, they'd only lived half of an expected life.

Three young soldiers didn't even have that. They'd left behind parents, brothers, sisters and girlfriends. Gone was their energy, their humour, their mateship. Bright futures, snuffed out but never forgotten.

Andy continued to play the mournful song as the casket of the mid-thirties mum went before him. Her three-year old daughter wouldn't understand that her mother wasn't coming home to her. Not in the way she was expecting. Hers was the last one.

Andy followed behind the procession, gently squeezing the bag for a smooth sound while his boots performed the precise movements of a slow march. The corridor seemed endless at a hundred metres.

Commanders still saluted, tears streaming down their faces.

Shock rippled through Andy and his fingers almost fumbled over a note. He'd never seen emotion or vulnerability in commanders to this degree.

White vans waited at the edge of the tarmac. Usually used for transporting aircraft parts, they'd been cleared out for more important cargo. Andy exhaled one last breath before striking the bag again to cleanly cut the music. Compared to the loud bagpipes, the silence that followed deafened.

He fought to keep his composure. Sounds of sobbing gently surrounded him as the soldiers farewelled their mates. Andy nodded to himself. He'd done his job.

The vans drove towards the morgue and the parade was dismissed. Several people thanked Andy for his contribution, but a numbness had swallowed him. Did he acknowledge them? He couldn't tell.

Everyone left and still Andy stood feeling empty and numb. A sob ripped through him and he shoved it back down. Men don't cry. His thoughts flashed to the commanders with their tear-streaked faces, and he was shocked anew. He kept seeing the caskets in his mind, thinking of the individuals and his heart cried out for the loss. An emptiness consumed him and with it an overwhelming grief he couldn't process.

Memories of another red and white draped casket flooded his mind leaving him raw. Megsy. His mate. Andy's legs crumpled underneath him, and he sat numbly on the tarmac surrounded by darkness.

———

ALARMS BLARED THROUGH THE PLANE. FEAR SETTLED LIKE A PIT IN Andy's stomach. What was going on? The aircrew all turned pale, their joking and camaraderie silenced as panic like a visible wave washed over them. "What's happening?"

Fearful eyes met his. "There are two missiles on our tail."

Training took over as someone called out, "Flares released."

"Get the parachutes," Another voice yelled from the cockpit as they suddenly nose-dived.

Andy jerked up from his seat as hands shoved him towards the back exit. "The chutes are at the back."

The normally level floor was tilted at a steep angle. He sprinted up the fuselage as fast as he could, but there was no traction.

"Go! Go!" The person behind him pushed again, but still he made no headway. The parachutes. He had to get the parachutes.

Why had he said 'yes' to go with the P-3 Orion? Sometimes an Avionics Technician like himself went with the aircraft to monitor a recent upgrade to the electronics. It was normally a long ride of nothing. As usual, when Andy was bored, he joked and teased his colleagues. They'd already made him airsick as payback for some of his comments.

But the lingering nausea lost the battle with the icy cold grip fear had on him. He pumped his arms harder. His thighs and calves burned with the effort to sprint up the steep incline.

"Where are they?" he asked his mate behind him when he finally reached the rear.

A cupboard was opened and a parachute thrust into his chest. His hands trembled as he tried to make sense of the package. He'd skydived solo before, but the training was too long ago. His shaky legs stepped into the gaps and he pulled the harness up over his camouflage uniform.

Time slowed to increments as flashes of his childhood played like a movie in his mind. His Army Infantry days and meeting his wife, Tina, at an Army Reserves Training course for the Sydney Olympics. His heart beat frantically. Was it remembering how fast it beat the first time he first saw her? The flashes of scenes continued to play. Their whirlwind romance. Transferring from the Army to the Royal Australian Air Force because of his mistaken idea that Tina would leave him. The marriage ceremony and the birth of their son, Lachie. His beautiful wife and son stayed in his mind. Would he get back home to them? A sorrowful ache at leaving them behind ripped at his heart.

The plane swung to the left and his stomach revolted. The whites of his knuckles stood out as he fisted the railing, waiting to be told to jump into enemy territory.

Where death would be the best thing to happen. He'd seen and tasted torture before.

Experiences with an exercise gone wrong, and assisting with Special Forces sent ideas of what lay ahead burrowing into his mind.

The thought of being blown out of the sky both appealed and repelled him.

Maybe he should hope for the quick death, but thinking he'd never see his family again devastated him. He would fight for them. For his mates. His infantry training surged to the forefront.

The alarms shut off, but their echo continued in his brain.

A call traveled the length of the plane. "The flares got one of the missiles and the other one was miles away."

Cheers sounded around him. Andy drew in an uneven breath and held it. His mate slapped him on his back and the air rushed out. He laughed. The missiles weren't even close. He busied his hands to stop their trembling.

Later, after disembarking with the air crew, word came that another Ramp Ceremony was scheduled. Dread seeped into his bones.

Andy flopped back onto his mattress and let the air-conditioner cool him down. It was an honour to serve by playing the pipes for the fallen, but he would rather be on that plane again facing his own mortality than play another Ramp for the dead.

<hr>

Adelaide, South Australia
September, 2008

Tina stepped through the doorway of the hall where the Elizabeth City Pipe Band practiced twice a week. It was the only time she had that was just for her. While Andrew played the bagpipes, she preferred the tenor drum and had a natural talent for flourishing and twirling the sticks. She just wished that she enjoyed it more. Playing with the band took up a lot of time, especially on weekends through spring and into summer. Since she didn't want to be left at home with Lachie, she joined in.

It had become her life-line—of sorts—while Andy was on deployment. Her dad arrived, like he did every week, after Lachie went to sleep at 7pm. It was her chance to get away from being a parent and just be herself.

She nodded a greeting to the pipers in the main hall who caught her eye and awkwardly waved before heading towards the room the drummers practiced in.

The drumming volume increased as she opened the door. Her fellow drummers all sat around the kid's tables grouped in the middle of the room.

"Hey! It's Lachie's Mum," the Pipe Sergeant, Daniel, greeted her, putting down his sticks.

Tina rubbed absently at her chest. So much for getting away from motherhood. She smiled weakly in return. "Hey."

"Lachie down for the night?"

"Yeah, he's really good at going to sleep." Her firmness at bedtime was the only hope she had for sanity.

Before she could change the subject, Daniel asked, "Have you heard from Andy?"

The worry that had plagued her all week rose up again, winding itself through her belly. "No, I haven't heard from him for a few weeks now." She forced a bright tone into her voice, "But I'm sure he's okay." He had to be. Tina refused to think about any other option. "What are we working on tonight?"

The practice went for another hour or so, and by the end, Tina was more than ready to go home. Why wasn't this restful? This is what she did to have time to herself. It's why her dad,

Robert, came over to watch Lachie. But it was just another place that she had to pretend that everything was okay.

Tina quietly opened the front door, not wanting to wake up Lachie. Her dad was on the lounge watching the TV. "Thanks, Dad." Guilt weighed on her shoulders as she saw him barely able to keep his eyes open. "If this is too much, just let me know. I don't want to take advantage."

He heaved up from the couch and waved away her concerns. "It's fine. Lachie's been asleep the whole time, I've just sat on my butt watching TV. I do that at home. I may as well do that here."

She rubbed his arm. "Thanks Dad. I really appreciate it." She hugged him tight and held the door as he left into the night.

Ring-ring!

Tina raced through the house. The phone rang again. She side-stepped the toys littered on the floor, her own personal obstacle course. *Ring-ring!*

Shooting through the doorway to the open plan living area, she lunged for the phone before it could wake Lachie.

"Hello?"

"Hi, honey." Andy's tired voice flowed down the line. Warmth spread through her and a little light in her soul flared back to life at the sound of her husband's voice. Relief soon followed, it had been too long this time between calls.

"Hey. It's good to hear your voice," she said, walking back through the obstacle course to the lounge room. "It's been a while, I was starting to get concerned. I know you guys aren't close to the action, but when I hadn't heard from you for— what? Three weeks now?"

Sounds of Andy clearing his throat had her pulling the phone away from her ear slightly. "Yeah. Sorry about that."

"Has it been busy, is that why you haven't called?"

"I've had a lot of 'ramps' to do."

What did that have to do with not calling her? She wasn't a needy person. She'd heard some married couples talked several times a day, but she had trouble thinking of what to talk about once a week. Her day to day caring for Lachie? She loathed boasting about milestones Andy was missing out on. Books she was reading? He hated the activity. That was the extent of her life. But even with nothing to talk about, she still needed to hear his voice occasionally. To know that her husband was okay. Alive. How had wives managed it during the World Wars? To live with that uncertainty every day? She focused on his words. "How many is a lot?"

He exhaled sharply into the phone. "I had one a few weeks ago that was six caskets. That was just one. We've been doing ramps and repatriation ceremonies two-to-three times a week." The gruff tone concerned her.

"That's when you're playing your pipes for the caskets coming into the base? Then after the plane's refueled, they return back to their country. Is that right?" The complex names and acronyms were sometimes hard to keep track of. But that was part of being a military spouse.

"Yeah. Ramps are when they come into base and Repatriation are when they leave to go home." He cleared his throat again. "They're hard to do."

She wasn't sure she understood why, so she asked, "What's so hard about it?"

"It's just constant. We're getting a lot of them. Not ours, but Canadians." His voice hitched on the last word.

"So, because you have to do so many of them, it makes it hard to do?" She felt stupid cause she still didn't get it.

An edge crept into his tone. "I get to know each person I'm playing for. That's how Marshall Snr taught me to play, with feeling." Every word is bit out. "I get to know the solider who fell so their friends can mourn, and then I pipe again when they leave to go home to their country. We send them off, and then the next day I'm sitting in the mess trying to eat breakfast while the Canadian news footage has the plane arriving on home soil. I get to see the families torn up as they meet the plane and the casket of their husband, their son, their father. The one I just piped for. I do that up to three times a week."

She had no words. Silence stretched between them. "Is there someone that you can talk to about it?"

Andy laughed joylessly. The dark tone chilled her. "I'm emailing Father Mark."

Something eased within her, at least he was talking to someone. "That's good. I'm glad you're talking to someone. Is it helping?"

That chilling laugh again. "Maybe if it was one Ramp, but they just keep coming. There's no end. It's the peak fighting time, so it probably won't let up until the end of my deployment."

She didn't know what to say.

"How's Lachie?"

She latched onto the new topic and prattled on, trying to disguise the unease his words had evoked. From the sounds of the odd 'uh-uh', he wasn't really listening to her anyway. Lachie was on a routine. He was good. She couldn't tell him that she was struggling to cope. That she was at the end of herself. He would worry for her if she told him how she really was.

Shaking off the disturbing thought, silence filled the line. How long had it been silent? "So, uh, yeah. That's us."

Andy cleared his throat again. "Yeah. Okay."

"Did you want to try and Skype with Lachie before you come home, so that he'll remember your face?"

"Nah, you know I can't handle being able to see him and not be there."

She nodded uselessly. "I know. I just wanted to give you the option in case you changed your mind."

Another awkward pause. They weren't big phone conversationalists, but the silences were unusual.

"Well, I'd better go and get some sleep."

"Okay. Sure. Have a good sleep. And don't leave it so long before you call me again. I was starting to worry."

His husky-tired voice promised, "I'll call again next week. I might have some idea on when I'll be coming home."

Coming home. Soon, he'd be home and then maybe she could finally breathe.

She hung up the line, silently praying for her man.

Lachie cried out, jerking her to the moment. He'd been sick this week with a head cold. It was times like this when being the sole carer of a little one sucked. Her favourite phrase when Andy got home was going to be, "Tag. You're it." The idea of soon having someone to share the parenting load gave her hope.

Keeping the lights off, she leaned down into Lachie's cot and picked him up, cradling him as he drew out from her the comfort he needed.

Lachie snuggled into her chest and breathed a little easier, so she settled into the rocking chair, put her feet up on the matching footstool and rocked them both gently, feeling more energy draining from her with every sway until all that was left was a bone-deep exhaustion.

She loved her son deeply and he loved her. It was just killing her slowly. A tear crept its way down her face. She didn't know how single parents managed. At least she had hope in Andy's return and this struggle wasn't going to be forever. Soon Andy would be home, and together they would do this parenting thing.

October, 2008

TINA GUIDED LACHIE'S SMALL HAND THROUGH THE GAP IN THE SEAT belt.

"Daddy?" Lachie asked, clutching his favourite Thomas the Tank Engine train.

"Yep, that's right, sweet, we're going to get Daddy from the airport." Tina couldn't contain the grin. It felt like forever since they'd been able to hug Andy. She clicked the seatbelts into the holder, tested for firmness and gave Lachie his sippy cup.

She drummed her fingers on the steering wheel as she pulled out onto the highway towards the city. How was Lachie going to react to his father? Nearly four months absence was an eternity to a toddler.

On their last phone call, Tina warned Andy that Lachie might not respond how he'd like when they reunited. She wasn't sure he understood. Her mind wandered to Lachie running and launching into Andy's arms. She smiled wryly and scoffed to herself, *That's not going to happen.*

Lachie was a clingy boy. Whether it was Andy's first tour not long after his birth that triggered it, or it was simply his personality, Tina doubted they would ever know the cause.

What she did know was that Lachie wouldn't be separated from her. He sought her attention and affection all the time and she didn't have much left in her to give.

That's why she hoped her little man would connect with his father again.

"Wiggles?"

Tina glanced at Lachie in the revision mirror. "Sure, sweetheart. Big Red Car?"

"Yep."

Tina sang along to the children's songs the rest of the way. After parking, she pulled out the puppy backpack that doubled as a safety harness and mentally rolled her eyes. Lachie was under her feet so often it was a wonder he wasn't covered in her footprints.

Excitement buzzed through her as they made their way through the safety stations and checked the board for the gate.

As they passed the large windows, the lights lit up the enormous aircraft waiting outside.

Lachie reached across her to point. "Panes."

"Yep, they're big planes aren't they? Daddy's coming on a big plane like that."

"Daddy pane?"

"No, sweetheart, that one isn't Daddy's plane." Tina hoisted him to her other hip as they turned right past the kiosk and made their way to the gate.

"Here we are," she sing-songed.

"Here we are." Lachie parroted as she set him to his feet. "Wook." He examined her face and pointed again.

Tina made a show of watching the workmen doing their jobs before smiling back at him. For once, he looked younger than his two years in his polar fleece onesie pyjamas. Andy had tried to get Tina to stay home. He'd wanted to take a taxi again because he didn't want to disturb Lachie's bedtime routine.

She was determined to welcome him home properly this time.

He didn't talk about it much, but she knew that the way his colleagues had come home last time from deployment had hurt. And the military were doing it to them again.

The Army and Navy would get news coverage when they returned home from deployment. Families all together, banners waved and cameras in faces. Honouring their service and celebrating their safe return.

Not the Royal Australian Air Force. They were told to come home in civilian clothes and brought home on different flights. Told to blend in and not draw attention to themselves. It was for their protection. But it felt as if the servicemen and women were ashamed of their part in the war.

So, Tina had decided that she and Lachie would be the welcoming party.

Maybe Andy would adjust back to regular life better than last time.

A plane came towards the gate and Tina took Lachie over to the large window to watch it come in.

"I think that one might be Daddy's plane." Tina knelt down and pointed in front of Lachie's face so he could see which one she meant. Lachie turned to her and babbled in his baby-talk. She nodded and smiled in supposedly all the right places. He lost interest the longer the aircraft took and Tina sat down on the conjoined seating.

She watched Lachie as he drove his train on the seats opposite and along the ground to her.

Always back to her. She was his everything. *Hopefully, not for much longer.*

He drove the train up her jean-clad leg. Tina rested her heel on the floor to stop the jiggling of her knee. She wasn't aware she'd been doing it.

Anxiety and excitement bundled in a ball inside as she saw passengers alight from the plane.

A small crowd had gathered at the top of the ramp, but Tina didn't pick up Lachie. She didn't want to get in the way, just in case he wanted to dive towards his Daddy. Nervous energy thrummed through her.

Strangers flowed past as friends and loved ones welcomed them. It seemed like the entire plane had already exited. She got the flight details right, hadn't she? Her pulse spiked.

Wait. There.

Her face split into a grin as she saw Andy striding up the ramp, his backpack slung over his shoulder and the bagpipes case in his hand. "Look Lachie." She knelt down again. "There's Daddy! You see him?"

Lachie watched the last remaining people walking up the ramp, his little face looking a touch overwhelmed.

She waved at Andy and grabbed Lachie's hand to wave it too.

Andy grinned and waved back.

She led Lachie over to the top of the ramp, now grateful that the majority of people had already left to get their baggage. The last ten metres took forever.

Blinking back tears, Tina threw her arms around Andy and kissed him soundly. She stepped back and tried to draw Lachie away from behind her leg. "Lachie, here's your daddy. Do you remember Daddy?"

Lachie buried his face in her jeans.

There was a sharp exhale like from a gut punch. She glanced up, catching the hurt and rejection on Andy's face.

"Come on, sweetheart, you remember Daddy." Tina tried tugging him again.

"It's fine. Don't force him." Andy knelt down to Lachie's height. "Hey, little man, I missed you. I see you brought Thomas with you." The thick words sounded strangled.

Lachie peered out from behind Tina and gazed seriously at his dad. He looked down at the Thomas in his hand and back up to Andy. "Thomath."

"How about if Daddy holds your tail, Lachie?" Tina asked, the hopeful tone obvious even to her own ears.

"No."

Tina's heart sank.

"Its fine. I've got stuff to carry, anyway. I think I need a trolley." Andy picked up the bagpipes case he'd left on the floor. "They said our things would be at baggage area two."

"That's this way. We walked past it on our way in." Tina picked up the backpack and unnecessarily took hold of the puppy's tail.

FIRE ERUPTED IN HIS CHEST AS ANDY GAZED AT HIS YOUNG SON. The rejection hurt, even though he tried to hide it. It wasn't a surprise Lachie wouldn't have anything to do with him. It was the second time in his short life that he'd abandoned his son. Guilt weighed him down more than the bags. He rolled his shoulders.

"You sure I can't take any of your bags?" Tina asked. He studied the face he loved. One he not too long ago he wasn't sure he'd see again.

"Nah, it's fine." He couldn't burden her with more than what she was already carrying. He reached out with his free hand and threaded their fingers together.

"How long was your flight? You only said what time to pick you up in the text message."

He rolled his eyes. "I've been travelling for about 32 hours. We travelled halfway around the country before we got here." Darwin, Townsville, Sydney. Waiting on the plane in Townsville while the uniformed Army members received their official welcome home by families and media before he was allowed to disembark.

He looked around, only one other family and no media. Not honoured by exiting the plane first. He nodded in his mate's direction. "They told us to wear civvies." A hard edge cut through his tone. He hated how it all made him feel—like dirt. As if serving their country was something to be ashamed of, or that the critical air support was deemed insignificant. Vietnam all over again.

"What? That's ridiculous."

He squeezed her hand. "Yep."

Andy drew in a deep breath and followed the signs to baggage area two.

Scanning the crowd, he pulled his little family over to the wall. "Wait here, I'll get a trolley."

Tina fished around in her purse for the gold coin required. "I can go, I don't mind."

"It will be too difficult with Lachie." *He won't want to stay here with me anyway.* His heart pierced and he rubbed the ache in his chest.

Andy walked over to the trolley rack and inserted the coin into the last one. He was so tired. It seemed like forever since he'd boarded the first flight leaving the Middle East, and yet, like it had only been a blink of an eye. Gone were days of soldiers and airmen taking weeks to travel home from war. After his last deployment, he wondered if that was a good thing or not. It was great to see his family so soon after his tour of duty, but... He worried about the nightmares. Perhaps if he'd had more time to process before coming home, they wouldn't still have their grip on him.

He'd tried to talk the psychologist at his Post Operation Psych. His mind flashed to the moment. He'd sat with the psychologist and started to tell him about the nightmares from the playing his pipes at the Ramps. The 'what did you do that for?' scathing response shocked. So, he clammed up. No one was going to help him. Without professional help to fight this, he was alone.

He ran his gaze over the crowd. Uneasiness squirmed inside with so many people around. The country felt strange, but familiar. He'd had stopovers in Kuwait, Maldives, Diego Garcia, Darwin, Townsville, Brisbane and Sydney. It would take some time to settle back in.

"Do you want to head over to the conveyor belt and wait for your things? You must be keen to get home," Tina asked as she looped an arm around his waist.

He sighed in pleasure and pulled her firmly in. "I'll wait here for the crowd to die down first. The bags will keep going around until I get them anyway."

Tina snuggled into his arms and they both looked down at Lachie driving his train along the base of the trolley.

The people thinned out until there was only a handful left. He pushed the luggage cart towards the conveyor belt, loaded his numerous bags and headed home.

2

Tina grinned and headed back to her room from tucking Lachie in. Their room. She had missed the close intimacy of their relationship.

"Lachie's asleep?" Andy asked as he finished unpacking his bags.

"He will be. He puts himself to sleep. I just read him stories and tuck him in." She sat on the now-cleared bed, beckoned Andy closer and entwined her arms around his neck. He didn't need further invitation and swooped down to kiss her.

A little while later, she pulled him back onto her bare chest. He rested his head over her heart.

"I missed you."

"I missed you, too."

Wet patches on her skin alerted her. "Is everything okay?" She tried to look in his face, but the darkened room prevented her from seeing him fully.

He cleared his throat, "Yeah, why?"

"You're crying."

"Nah. I'm just tired. You know how my eyes leak when I yawn."

"Mm." Tina wasn't convinced. "If there *is* anything, you can tell me."

"Yeah, I know."

They lay in silence.

"I, uh, I've been having nightmares." His arms tightened around her.

"What about?"

"Oh, just stuff that happened. I played the bagpipes for the Ramp Ceremonies. I dream about them."

Tina scanned her brain and cursed her terrible memory. "What's a ramp ceremony again?"

"When they bring the bodies of the fallen soldiers off the plane. They have a ceremony."

"Why's it called a 'Ramp' Ceremony?"

"'Cause of the ramp on the plane."

"Oh. Of course." Her heart thumped with sadness. "I'm not surprised you have nightmares. It's emotional."

Andy tightened his grip again and she clung to him. It seemed as if he was in a turbulent ocean and she was the only life buoy in sight.

Except she wasn't a life buoy. She was another swimmer battling to keep her own head above water. Was it possible to drown in love? She was slowly drowning in Lachie's need for her. She knew Who could help, because her Saviour was the only one keeping her head over the thrashing waves of depression.

"Have you spoken to anyone about it?" *Pot, this is Kettle,* she thought. A nasty tone crept into her mind. *Talking, what's that going to do? Not that you'd know.* Her own failure to get help engulfed her with shame.

"I emailed Father Mark a lot while I was over there."

She smiled. "He told me that at church one Sunday. He said that you were processing stuff with him?"

"Yeah. He was a safe place to talk."

"Did it help."

She felt him snort. "Yeah. Kind of." He paused. "Not really. It was too intense while I was there."

His words broke her heart. "Did you talk to anyone else? A counsellor?"

"I spoke with the psych at the POP - the Post Operational Psych review." He knew her too well. "I told them that I offered to play the bagpipes for the ceremonies and that I was now having nightmares about it." He scoffed. "They said, 'What did you do that for?'"

Fury swelled inside her but she squelched it down. Rage wasn't what he needed from her, but empathy for the injustice. A little indignation slipped out. "That's awful! What right do they have to say that? They're supposed to help you. What are you going to do now?"

She felt the shrug of his shoulder. "I don't know. I can't talk to anyone. I'm alone."

"You're not alone. I'm here. God's always with you."

"You can help." Hope brightened his voice.

Tina pictured the ocean and the buoy again. She wasn't the buoy. She was right next to him, drowning too. Her hope of sharing the parenting load had fizzled into ash. Andy needed more time to adjust being home. Could she tread water long enough to wait? The darkness threatened to take over.

"I can listen when you want to talk, and I can love you. But I can't save you." She hoped he didn't hear the slight panic in her voice. "I can't fix what's broken inside you. Only Jesus can do that. I'm not God."

Silence ballooned into the atmosphere, heavy with all that he didn't say.

Her heart broke at the mess they were both in. *Save us, Jesus, only You can fix this.* She snuggled deeper in his arms, careful to take deep breaths so he wouldn't notice the wet slide of tears on her cheeks.

***

THE KETTLE FINISHED BOILING AS TINA REMOVED THE RECYCLING
bin from its holder and went out the kerbside bins next to the
garage. Lachie followed as usual. She couldn't go anywhere
without her little suffocating shadow. The ever-present sadness
tried to breach the mask she wore. She couldn't risk letting the
pretense go while Andy was home.

She upended the recycling contents, flinching at the sound of
glass bottles crashing together. She peered into the bin. There
were a lot of wine bottles hiding under the paper rubbish. All red.
She didn't drink red wine, only Andy and her dad. She counted a
couple of whisky bottles too. How much was Andy drinking after
she went to bed?

Her brow furrowed as she returned inside, replacing the bin
and setting the kettle to boil. Again. Should she say something?
Was he going to end up like one of the Vietnam veterans who
turned to alcohol to deal with their issues after the war? She
didn't want that. Not for him, and not for their family. Lachie
needed a father. One that was involved in his life, not watching
from the sidelines.

She opened the fridge and peered inside. Not enough milk.
Having another person in the house again completely threw her
routine out. She exhaled loudly and strolled towards the lounge
room where Andy was sprawled on the couch.

Her legs bent forward as a little bundle of energy crashed into
her from behind. She reached down to smooth Lachie's hair. "It's
alright, darlin'. I just need to talk to Daddy." She shook her head
and sighed again. She'd only left the kitchen. When was Lachie
going to be okay with being alone with Andy again? Was she
enabling the behaviour? It had been two months since Andy
returned home, but Lachie only showed a little interest in him in
the last couple of days.

Lachie let go of her leg and followed her through the open
hall.

Maybe if she went out and left them together, they'd sort it out. The pressure and weight on her shoulders lightened for a moment. She was so tired of pretending everything was okay. Her facade was beginning to show cracks since Andy had returned.

"Hey, hon, I just need to duck out to the shops and get some milk. I'll leave Lachie here with you."

"Will he be okay?"

Tina frowned slightly in consideration, "Yeah, he should be. He doesn't have daytime naps anymore and he's had lunch." She shrugged. "If he's hungry, just get him a snack from the pantry. His sippy cup is in the family room if he's thirsty. I shouldn't be gone long."

Tina headed to the bedroom, put on her shoes and collected her bag.

Lachie was driving another train along the queen-sized bed. "Lachie." She met his gaze. "I'm just going to the shops to get some milk, sweetheart. Daddy will stay here with you." Grabbing the car keys, she ducked to the front door just outside the bedroom as his tears began.

She threw herself out the door and mentally braced for the screaming. *He'll be okay. He'll be okay. They need this. I need this*, she chanted to herself. She wasted no time in pointing the car to her favourite shopping centre.

What kind of a mother are you, leaving your screaming baby? A voice taunted in her head. Hers? Something else? *He'll be okay. It might take Lachie five minutes to stop crying, but he will. Andy will settle him and they can build their relationship.*

The car park was reasonably busy being a Saturday afternoon, but it still didn't take more than a minute to find a park. Tina straightened out of the car and headed to the entrance. *Nobody knows me. I can let my facade down and stop pretending.* The automatic doors opened and Tina let it all hang out.

Sadness engulfed her and she fought back tears. People passing looked at her strangely, but she didn't care. What was wrong with her? She had everything. A beautiful family, a home, family living close by. Friends at church. Food. Why wasn't she happy? Staying at home full time with Lachie was her choice. But he was killing her slowly in love. It felt like he was suffocating her, each breath a fight.

Dawdling, Tina grabbed the milk. She stared vacantly, the cold air rushing out of the open door while she wondered at the level of the other milk they used. She reached for two litres of Lachie's special milk. Each step to the checkout felt like walking through mud, yet too quickly she found herself on the way back towards the automatic doors.

Tina dragged her feet as the doors approached and sighed again heavily. A man came from behind and walked through the doors in front of her.

He caught her attention when he turned around. He leaned in close, and Tina automatically pulled back. "Smile," he said.

"I'm sorry?" Her eyebrow arched. Why was a strange man telling her to smile?

He backed out of her personal space and shifted his shopping to his other hand. Tina kept moving hoping the stranger would continue on.

He turned and walked with her into the car park. "I saw you when you came into the shops earlier and you looked so sad. I wanted you to smile."

Horror swept through her. No one was supposed to notice, let alone call her out on it. She plastered a smile on her face. "I'm fine. Truly. I don't know why you would think I was sad." The false brightness almost made her cringe.

"It caught my attention 'cause my friend just died, and you looked how I feel."

She slowed to a stop. "Oh no, I'm so sorry to hear that."

The man looked around and lowered his voice. "He took his own life."

"That is sad." Compassion filled her. "Is there a funeral, will you be able to go and say goodbye?"

He shook his head. "I can't make it, he lived in another state."

"Maybe there's something that you could do that will remind you of him, help you remember the good times."

He thought about it and smiled shyly, "I'm going to bake a cake." Enthusiasm warmed his tone. "I've never done it before, but he loved to cook."

"That's a great idea." The conversation continued until it grew awkward again. "Anyway, I need to get home before the milk warms up. Again, I'm sorry for your loss, but enjoy baking your cake in memory of your friend."

He nodded. "And you smile more."

They smiled farewell and Tina walked towards her car. She sat in the seat and closed the door, its loud bang entombing her within.

That was weird.

And horrifying. Weren't strangers supposed to pretend they didn't see you?

Tina rubbed her hand up and down her forehead.

The conversation with the stranger played on her mind all the way home and she prayed for the man. Now that was something to be sad about.

She reversed into the driveway and paused before undoing her seatbelt and mentally fixing her happy-go-lucky facade.

Andy met her at the door with a screaming Lachie. He thrust their son at her and she scrambled to grab him without dropping the milk. "He hasn't stopped since you left." Andy looked pale, like he was fighting back his own tears. She knew exactly how he felt. "Never do that to him again."

Tina nodded numbly and prised Lachie's arms from the stranglehold he had on her neck, hoisting him into a more comfortable position. "It's okay, Lachie. Mummy's home, like I promised. Daddy looked after you, didn't he." She made sure her tone was bright.

Lachie settled and admonished her with his tear-filled gaze. His blue eyes a replica of her own.

Her inner critic didn't waste the opportunity. *What a terrible mother. Dumping Lachie on his father when he'd only just started to be interested in knowing him. You've ruined their relationship. He won't want anything to do with Andy now. And you'll pay the price.*

The desire to escape from reality hit hard. Had she finished the stack of books from the library yet? She cuddled Lachie to her while she headed for the bag of books like an addict searching for the next fix. Settling Lachie in front of his favourite Thomas the Tank Engine DVD, she sat back on the futon, book in hand ready to open to the first page. She couldn't even be bothered reading the back again to find out what the story was about. Lachie climbed up next to her and snuggled while he watched.

Amused, and yet furious at the lack of space she desperately needed, Tina thrust open the book before either emotion erupted. The fury quickly faded. She couldn't be angry at her son for wanting love and attention. The sadness that always seemed to be around shadowed her soul, but soon she lost herself and her depressing reality in the scenes of pure escapism.

"HI, FATHER MARK." ANDY HEARD TINA'S GREETING AS SHE opened their front door. The words struck Andy with anxiety. Did he really want to share what was on his mind with a man of God?

He flexed his fingers, reminding him of the hat he'd had specially made for the priest. Exhaling out a breath, he turned the green cap with Padre embroidered on the back and ran his fingers over the pale yellow stitching.

Padre was the term the military used for the chaplains. He had no idea how the Spanish word for 'Father' was the common term, it just was. Father Mark didn't serve in any of the forces, and so he technically wasn't a Padre, but from the way he'd supported Andy on his deployment, Father Mark may as well have been.

His fingers trembled as a wave of emotions overwhelmed him. He might not have made it home to his family if not for the man of God.

Andy stood as Tina and Father Mark walked into the room. Without a word, Andy opened his arms and embraced his life line. The other man was around his own height, but older and his white and black speckled beard brushed against Andy's cheek. He closed his eyes to keep the tears at bay.

They pulled back and Andy untangled the cap from his fingers. "It took a bit longer than I wanted, but I got this made for you." He held out the hat.

Father Mark reached for it and met his eyes. "What's this for?"

"I wanted to thank you for everything that you did for me while I was deployed." His eyes skirted to Tina, watching him. "I, uh, wrote some dark stuff in those emails and I want to say thank you for being a safe place for me to vent."

Father Mark's expression softened. "I'm always here for you. I'm sorry that I couldn't do more."

Andy shook his head. "You were there. That's what I needed." He gestured to the back of the cap. "I had the stitch-bit—ah, the ladies who do the stitching at the clothing store—embroider 'Padre' on the back. It's what we call priests who serve in the military."

Father Mark smiled as he examined the word, his face lighting up. He met Andy's gaze. "Thank you, Andy. It means a lot to me." The depths reflected in his eyes.

Andy smiled in return. "There's only one of those. It's the same type of cap that we wear, but only yours has 'Padre'."

Father Mark cradled the cap to his chest, and pulled him in for another hug.

When they pulled apart, Tina offered them hot drinks. After she brought them to the dining table, she joined them. The conversation grew stilted.

After an awkward pause, Tina looked from him to Father

Mark and back again. "I might go and start putting dinner on, if you don't mind me leaving you to it."

As she left, Andy focused back on his friend. "You have no idea how much your emails meant to me." He glanced down at his coffee and tried to push the words past the lump in his throat. "I wrote you some pretty harsh things."

Father Mark listened as he poured out again what he saw, and how it affected him. Nightmares he didn't want to describe that kept him from sleep. The rage that dragged him deeper and deeper into this hole. But shame silenced him from sharing how he hid in the shower to cry tears that refused to stop. From facing the growing hatred towards Muslims and the whole Middle East.

After a long pause, Father Mark answered, "I'm so sorry for what you've been through. I can't imagine what it was like. I'm happy to listen to you whenever you want to talk, Andy, but I'm not a counsellor. I don't have the tools to help you."

Sorrow filled Andy as yet another avenue evaporated in front of him. The psychs wouldn't help. Tina couldn't help. And now a man of God couldn't help. The turbulent thoughts surrounded him, leaving him alone in an endless ocean of pain.

TINA WRAPPED THE BLANKET TIGHTER AROUND HER BODY AND snuggled deeper into the futon. Not that it was cold in late spring, but there was nothing wrong with curling up with a good book.

Except when it's all you do, a nasty voice pointed out. She'd been hearing it more often lately, since that day at the shops a few weeks ago.

She tried to ignore the inner critic. Reading was her escape.

Lachie had recently eaten lunch, so she should be fine to lose herself in the romance novel for a couple of hours. The new Thomas train was set out, and that would amuse him for hours. It was the only thing he played with that he didn't demand interaction with her.

Not that she had anything left to give him anyway.

The large stack of thick books she'd already read that week sat in the bag beside the couch, a testament to how much she'd been escaping lately.

The words on the page soon drew her and the fairytale began. Boy meets girl, they don't want to like each other but they do. Steamy scenes, and before long heartbreak. The world tuned out until a cry caught her attention.

It took a few moments for Tina to focus on her surroundings. Lachie had thrown himself over her legs and started talking in his baby garble. Irritation swept through her. It was the good bit in the story.

She snapped like a rubber band stretched too thin.

"Lachie!" She yelled into his little face. "Can't you see I'm busy? What do you want?"

His little face paled and his eyes widened before filling with tears. He ran away.

Shame filled her.

He came back carrying his empty sippy cup.

Guilt attacked her and she doubled over.

He wanted a drink. Her baby wanted a drink and she yelled at him, right in his little face.

What kind of mother are you? The voice criticised her again.

She tried to ignore it.

Tina drew Lachie into her arms. "I'm so sorry, sweetheart." She rocked him backwards and forwards. "Mummy's so sorry."

She took the sippy cup and shifted him onto her hip. "Do you want some milk?" Her voice cracked.

He held himself away from her and stared into her face. Not meeting her eyes.

She blinked back the tears that threatened to course down her cheeks.

Lachie nodded. "Milk."

By the time she'd given him milk, he'd forgiven her. If only it was that easy to forgive herself.

"Do you want to watch some Thomas?" Tina asked as she led him through to the lounge room.

"Thomath," Lachie replied.

She put the DVD on for him, waited until he was absorbed in the Island of Sodor before heading back into the family room. She sunk onto the futon and let the tears flow.

A good mother would never do that to her child, the voice taunted.

Tina grabbed the cushion and sobbed silently into its softness. She was a terrible mother.

You should go stick your head in the oven, it tempted her.

Should she?

The pain will go away, it promised.

There's got to be a better way to do it.

Just do it now.

Her chest tightened and her breath arrested.

What about my family? She choked on her held breath. What about Lachie? She couldn't do that to him. Couldn't take away his mother, even if she was a terrible one. There were too many stories of people who suffered because they didn't have someone who loved them. The idea of Lachie growing up without a mum filled her eyes again. No. This wasn't going to happen.

The air seemed to momentarily lighten at her decision. She put the cushion down.

What now? There was no way out. Andy wasn't in any state to help her. And even though she knew something was wrong with him, she had nothing left to give him. She could barely even think of his issues because her own dominated. There was no help. No way of getting better.

The air grew heavy and dark with her thoughts. She didn't even know what was wrong with her. All she knew was she loved her son so much, but he was slowly and silently drowning her in his need for her focus. How could she deny him?

She grew tired of trying to keep her head above water, but

still, she gave more and more until she was nothing but an empty shell.

Where are you, God? Can you even hear me? What's wrong with me?

A sense of comfort pierced the darkness that covered her soul. Words floated within. *Post Natal Depression.*

I can't have Post Natal Depression. Lachie is two! I didn't match any of the symptoms on the website last time I looked. I'm not depressed. I'm just sad, really, really sad.

But the words 'Post Natal Depression' seemed to linger in her soul with a sense of certainty.

Unsure what to do with that or how it could even help, Tina got up off the futon even as her soul descended into her own personal darkness.

3

December, 2008

A ndy glared at the screen. The news highlights showed more footage of the war in the Middle East. More soldiers risking their lives. For what? The world was ungrateful for the help. Every one wondered why they were even there in the first place. Remarks about oil and greed pierced him, their words turning soldiers into mercenaries.

Tina bent down in front of him to help Lachie pack away the train set sprawled all over the lounge room floor. He'd had to tiptoe past all the pieces when he got home from work, irritating him.

Lachie named all the trains as he put them in the box. Andy was a little surprised a two-year old knew them all. He couldn't keep them all straight in his mind.

Lachie waddled over to show him the newest train they'd bought at the shops earlier. It was red.

"Jameth," Lachie said, extending it towards him.

Andy smiled. Lachie had gradually begun warming up to him. He still wanted Tina for everything, but at least Lachie acknowledged his presence.

Lachie climbed up on the lounge next to him and snuggled in. Andy froze, not wanting to scare him away.

He met Tina's hopeful expression.

"Lachie, would you like Daddy to come and join us for stories tonight?"

Lachie nodded.

Andy grinned. The desperate need to connect with his son flared to life. It had to be on Lachie's terms.

A little while later, Andy snuggled next to Lachie on the single bed. After the last story was read, Andy closed his tired eyes. The books had almost put him to sleep. He snuggled deeper into the blankets and Lachie wrapped his tiny arms around him.

Tina leaned over to kiss Lachie goodnight. "Good night, Lachie-bear." She snickered, "Night, honey." Her lips brushed his forehead. Cheeky. Moving took too much effort, so he let his heavy eyelids stay closed.

Andy jerked awake. The mutilated bodies from his nightmare lingered. He shook the gruesome scenes away, and peered behind the curtains at the full dark. His fingers fumbled for the button on the side of his watch to light it up. Nine o'clock. Andy untangled out of the blankets, careful not to wake the sleeping toddler next to him.

His face was rough under his palms as he rubbed it on the way to the kitchen. Grabbing a wine glass from the drainer, Andy poured himself a red wine. "Did you want a glass of wine?" He called out to Tina.

Silence.

What? Where was she?

Fear flicked his nerves. Had she left him again with Lachie? Or had something else… he couldn't bear to finish the thought.

He ducked his head around the doorway, seeing her curled up in the armchair, the book in her hands holding every bit of her attention.

He relaxed into the doorway, slumping against the frame and tried again. "Do you want a glass of wine?"

Still no answer.

"Tina."

She jerked up, blinking to focus on him. "Huh?"

He hated repeating himself, and her deep absorption in books that caused it. Argh. "I said, did you want a glass of wine?" Annoyance dripped from his tone.

"Sorry, honey. I didn't hear you." No joke. "I didn't think we had any," she added.

He strode back to the kitchen and stuffed the cork back in the bottle before heading back to the lounge. If she'd answered, he wouldn't have had to go back and forth like an idiot.

Andy stretched out on the couch and stole the remote. He flicked through the channels, not surprised Tina didn't complain. Yep. Head in a book again.

He settled on an American sitcom and took a long gulp of wine. By the end of his second glass the next show had finished, but he wasn't.

He caught Tina's worried glance before she focused on the TV screen. "Do you realise how much you've been drinking lately?" She asked, her tone curious instead of judgmental.

Guilt beat at him, but he held it back. "Yeah, it's fine. I'm okay."

She smiled a sad smile and relief threaded through him when she didn't press any further. He knew he was drinking more. There was a reason for it. Maybe if he drank enough the bodies wouldn't take over his sleep.

Another news highlight between the ad breaks. He couldn't get away from it, and yet the segments drew him in at the same time. They showed footage of the latest Ramp Ceremony. Vitriol spewed out of him, "Bloody waste of space. They should just nuke them all."

A gasp from the other side of the room reminded him he wasn't alone. "You don't mean that."

He pinned her with his gaze. "Yes, I do."

"What about all the women and children? The innocents? The war isn't their fault."

"They're all the same. You can't trust what they're wearing under their burkas, and they use the kids like in Vietnam."

Tina rubbed absently at her chest, a look of horror on her face. Well, war was horrific, and they should just bomb the lot of them. Then they'd be no more war. And no more soldiers dying.

He turned back to the TV, grateful the show had returned. The canned laughter from the audience out of place in the too-quiet room.

Tina said softly, almost under her breath, "You can't tarnish them all with the same brush. Not all Muslims are terrorists or are working for them."

"There's always collateral damage in war."

It wasn't long before Tina went to bed and he settled in to finish the bottle of wine, eyeing off the whisky he was yet to pour. The nap he'd had earlier would tide him over for a bit, but he wanted to pass out.

He'd do anything to prevent another nightmare.

Tina pushed the door open on her parents' house and Lachie stepped over the threshold.

"Poppy!" Lachie's high-pitched voice exclaimed his excitement for his pal.

Her dad grinned at her son and scooped him up into his arms. "Hey, Lachie-bear." The affectionate name for her son had become a family thing.

"Hey, Dad." Tina put the back pack down by the door and kissed her dad.

"Andy not coming?" Dad's blue eyes were puzzled.

"Nah, he needed some peace and quiet." She needed to get Lachie away from Andy's irritable mood. Again. It felt like two steps forward, three steps back.

She walked over to the coffee table and pulled out the train set.

Lachie kicked his legs to be put down, so Dad gently swooped him to the ground. Lachie took the lid off the black container and began putting the pieces together.

Rob's eyebrows shot up. "He's doing it by himself now?"

She grinned. "Yup. He can even get the two ends to join up." It still amazed her.

They watched for a few more seconds. "Is Andy okay? He hasn't been himself since he came home." Her father's words yanked her attention. Her lips tugged in a sad, half smile. He didn't miss much.

"Actually, Andy hasn't been the same since he left for his first tour." She took a deep breath to stop tears from forming. "War changed him. I don't know why, all I know is that the man that I married is not the same one that came home. It's more noticeable this time, and I think the Ramp Ceremonies had something to with it. He's not coping."

"I might see if he wants to go for a game of golf."

She screwed her face up. "Andy doesn't really play golf…"

He gave her a flat look. "While we're playing, I'll tell him that I'm here for him if he ever wants to talk."

Love for her dad warmed her, and she hugged him. "Thanks, Dad. I don't know if he'll open up, because he's not admitting, at least to me, that he has a problem. But I appreciate your offer, and I know he will."

Without her parents' support, she wouldn't have coped either. How long could they continue like this?

The thought of confronting Andy made her nervous, especially after the hatred he spewed last night like an erupting volcano. He tried to pretend he was okay, but she knew a facade when she saw one. She still wore hers every day.

If she wasn't ready to tell her family about her depression, she couldn't blame him for not wanting to talk about his problem.

THE NEXT DAY, TINA READ THE INSTRUCTIONS ON THE SMALL BOX and followed them.

She sat on the bed and waited.

Her thoughts churned. What if? What if not? Was she ready for this?

She checked the time. It hadn't even been a minute.

She couldn't do this. Panic filled her and she took a shaky breath.

Tina watched the stick, thinking her eyes must've tricked her. She'd done this before and she'd been mistaken. Looking so hard that she imagined what wasn't there. But she didn't imagine this.

The little stick had two blue lines.

She bolted up and paced the small space before the desk.

She'd wanted to have kids a little closer together in age, but with Andy's deployment they had no other choice than try for another baby straight away. Who would expect it to be this quick?

Their little family would grow.

She wasn't ready.

Wiping her sweaty palms against her clothes, she pulled up short.

I can't cope with one baby. What am I going to do with this new one? She needed help. She had to let someone in.

Tina sank on the bed and flopped backwards. What was Andy going to think?

He wasn't coping well. His comment the other night frightened and devastated her. His hatred hurt her heart.

Something was seriously wrong with him.

It wasn't like him at all.

God, what's going on with Andy?

Quiet words she didn't understand came to mind.

PTSD.

What's PTSD? She hadn't heard of it before. A vague memory surfaced - a segment of a news program about soldiers and PTSD.

She went to the computer and typed it into the search bar. A few clicks and a list for Post Traumatic Stress Disorder popped up on the screen.

Nightmares. Yep.

Easily angered or irritated. Yep.

She continued down and mentally checked off all but a couple of the symptoms. No flashbacks. No anxiety. At least not that she'd seen.

An unnamed tension released within. Post Traumatic Stress Disorder. Somehow having a name for what was happening to Andy made it easier to breathe.

Another memory from several years earlier rose to the front of her mind.

She'd been sitting on the bed reading her bible and the passage she'd read stood out. The words seemed brighter on the page. It was talking about going through a season so bad that one would want to die. She prayed because she *knew* that the passage related to Andy, and she'd clung to the hope at the end of the passage. That he would get through it. She hadn't known what it would mean other than the journey would be awful, but he would get through it.

Tina had felt it in her bones.

This was that journey.

Andy likely had Post Traumatic Stress Disorder, she had something like Post Natal Depression and a newborn on the way. Terror stole her breath. What were they thinking, how could they bring another life into this mess? The next moment, a calmness settled over her and she exhaled. She had to face herself and take away the mask. Her soul rebelled at being naked and vulnerable.

Tina's eyes bounced back to the two blue lines. New life was coming into their world. How did she want to welcome it? She couldn't handle another baby, not feeling so broken inside. Images flicked through her mind, instead of the loving and warm family she'd always dreamed of, visions of being an absent mother, sinking into a deep and dark depression that she'd never come out of.

Or she could tell someone. She tucked her knees into her chest and hugged them tight. Why was the thought so terrifying? She could tell her family, and get what she needed to get better. The warm and loving family she wanted might not be out of reach after all.

Resolve strengthened her.

It was time to get well so she could support Andy through the path ahead of them. Time to stop pretending. Andy didn't ask to have PTSD, like she didn't ask for her own mental health issues, and he needed her to be strong to fight alongside him.

If they were going to move forward from here... what would another deployment do to him?

Unease filled her. The squadron he was in were doing continuous rotations because the aircraft were so useful in the Middle East. They were stretched thin. He didn't want to go on the last deployment, but if he'd stayed home they would have sent someone else who had already been twice.

If he deployed a third time, she knew he wouldn't come back. Certainty filled her, although she didn't know how she could know. She simply knew. He had to post to another base. If they stayed... she forced her mind away from the thought.

Could she bring it up with Andy?

She sunk into the soft mattress. He wasn't admitting to her that he even had a problem. He wouldn't hear her if she told him her thoughts.

Tina mentally shook her head to clear it as Lachie wandered into the room. Thanks to his onesie pyjamas, his leg reached halfway up the bed, so she sat up to give his nappy-covered butt a boost. He was adorable. Her smile grew to a grin.

And soon they would have another one.

THE GARAGE DOOR SLID TO THE GROUND AND ANDY CAUGHT THE handle before it slammed to the ground.

"Daddy's home," Lachie called through the fly-screen door.

Another day almost done and then he just had to get through the next one. Rumours of another tour to the Middle East next year dominated his thoughts while anxiety skimmed along his nerves.

He grasped the door handle and stepped in the doorway, bracing himself for Lachie's hug. "Mummy." Lachie looked over his shoulder and pointed at him. "Daddy's home." He bent down and absently rubbed his son's back.

Andy watched Tina as she approached from the bedroom. "Hey, Honey. How was your day?" She leaned in for a kiss and he pecked her lips gently.

"There's rumours of another Middle East tour next year."

"Someone else will go though, right? You only just got back. It's gotta be another person's turn." Her brow furrowed in concern.

Everyone else had already been. Bleakness threatened to overwhelm him. He couldn't go back. Not again. But he shrugged, "I just know my name was bandied around." He put his key in the bowl and set down his bag.

Indignation flared in her eyes. "But you've already been twice. Why can't someone else go that's only been once."

He shrugged again, "There aren't many left who haven't been twice. A lot will have to go a third time." He clenched his fist to hide his trembling fingers.

Tina sat heavily on the bed. "But you've only just got back. Surely there are others that went on the previous rotation."

He pulled out his ID and set it next to the bowl of keys. He couldn't look her in the eye. He couldn't go back, he wouldn't survive another tour. He was still haunted by the last one. His head hung low and he pretended to search for something deeper in his bag. It was his duty to go, how could he send someone else in his place? But if he went, he would take his own life. His mind already planning the how.

The bag fell to the floor and he finally met Tina's eyes. They seemed to pierce deep into his soul. He was laid bare. He rubbed his face to break the connection.

"You know." She searched his eyes again when he dropped his hand. "I've been thinking we should move to Newcastle. Lachie barely knows your parents and, I hate to say it, but they're a lot older than Mum and Dad. They might not be around for much longer. I want Lachie to have a relationship with them. I barely know my grandparents 'cause we've always lived on the other side of the country. I don't want that for Lachie, or this baby." Her hand rested on her stomach.

What? Hope flared to life within but he didn't want to grab hold in case it was a mirage. "What about the MEAO?"

"They'll just have to send someone else."

"But it's my duty."

"You've done your duty. Two rotations is doing your duty. What about all the other AvTechs that want to go?"

He nodded. "There's a lot of complaining from the other Squadrons because they aren't getting to go, and we're getting burnt out."

"I can imagine. You can't be the only one that has had enough."

"There's been a couple of others that have posted out." The flame of hope grew brighter.

Tina gestured with her arm. "See? You need to get out of this place. It's not good for you to go back again." How did she know? It's like she knew he would take his life over there if he went again. "And I do want our kids to have a relationship with their grandparents. That's important to me." She paused, "Would they let you go?"

Would work let him go? "I'd have to ask for a compassionate posting, I think. We have a limited number we can use."

Her serious eyes met his. "I think this is the perfect time to use it."

Anything that stopped him from going back to the Desert.

Medowie, New South Wales
February, 2009

TINA BROUGHT THE STEAMING MUGS OF TEA AND COFFEE TO THE dining room table where Andy and Leonie, her mother's best friend, were talking.

"Thank you, darlin'." Leonie reached out for her mug.

Tina went back to the kitchen, but threw over her shoulder, "You're welcome." She grabbed her own mug of herbal tea, holding her mostly flat stomach as she eased onto the chair. Lachie trailed along behind. He'd been a little more attached than usual since the move to Medowie, near Newcastle in the Lower Hunter.

"So, what made you both decide to leave Adelaide? I thought you had planned on settling there. I know Kathy and Rob were expecting you to stay longer." Leonie asked before sipping from her tall mug.

Tina caught Andy glancing her way before he answered Leonie. "We decided that my parents are getting older and we want Lachie and the new baby to get to know their other grandparents."

"It sounds terrible to say it"—Tina interjected—"but since Mum and Dad are a lot younger than Andy's parents, it's more likely that Andy's Mum and Dad won't be around as long for the kids to get to know them." Tina drew in her lower lip and shrugged slightly. "I didn't really know my grandparents 'cause they lived on the other side of the country. We don't want that for Lachie or the baby."

Leonie took a sip of her hot tea. "What about your parents

though, Tina, didn't they move to Adelaide to be close to you guys?"

"Yeah, that's what made the move so hard. It broke my heart to leave them there, but we needed to go." That was the reason they were telling everyone, at least. Tina looked deep into her mug and cupped her hands around its warmth. "Like we said, Andy's parents aren't getting any younger. Mum and Dad can Skype, but Andy's parents can't do that for themselves."

The conversation flowed with another cup of tea. Tina returned to the dining room in time to hear Leonie talk about Christmas just past. Her face lit up, animated with her passion for her faith. "… Don't you just love the hope that we have?"

Andy's eyes had glazed over.

Tina blinked back the tears that threatened. He'd believed too. Before. She sighed. But she'd rescue him from a conversation he didn't want.

She resumed her seat. "I don't get it."

Leonie frowned slightly and tilted her head. "What do you mean?"

She shrugged. "I don't get it. I understand that the bible says that Jesus is the hope of the world. But I don't get it. What is hope?" Tina pressed her lips together. She hadn't meant to reveal that. She'd tried to save Andy and threw herself in it instead.

Lachie tugged on her arm, and she focused on him, grateful for the interruption.

"Excuse me a minute." She let Lachie drag her to her room where a toy had disappeared under her bed. She retrieved it and after sending Lachie back on his way, she sat heavily on the bed.

Tell her. A quiet yet insistent voice urged.

I can't. What would I say? I feel like I'm wearing a cloak of sadness? That just sounds ridiculous.

Tell her.

No, I can't tell her. Maybe God would compromise. *What if I show her? I'll drop the facade and if she notices, then I know that I'm supposed to say something.*

Exhaling sharply, Tina slumped her shoulders. I don't want to. Tina straightened her back. *I can't continue this way.*

Right. The facade was coming down.

She returned to the table where Leonie sat talking with Lachie about his toy. Andy had retreated to the lounge, the talk about God probably chased him away.

Leonie leaned forward and clasped Tina's hand. "What did you mean about not 'getting' hope?"

Tina shrugged. She met Leonie's gaze and for a split second dropped her mask. The sadness, the despair, covering her. "I don't understand what hope is." It was hard to describe something that you once experienced, but was unable to remember. "I know that I used to get it, but I don't anymore. I don't have any hope."

Leonie reached out and covered Tina's hands with her other one, encasing them. "Jesus is our hope." She reassured with a quiet certainty.

Tina shrugged, pulling her hands away and changed the subject. She felt stripped naked, and even though she knew Leonie loved her, she couldn't bear to feel so exposed.

Leonie stood up a while later and took Tina's hand again. "Can I speak to you in private for a minute, Tina, before I leave?"

A strange feeling welled up within. "Of course."

"Can we go into your room?"

The feeling grew. She nodded and led the way.

Tina sat on the bed and Leonie closed the door and sat next to her, "Tina, is everything okay?"

"Why? What do you mean?" Tina's voice was high-pitched to her own ears. Her heart raced.

Leonie eyes filled with compassion. "When you were talking earlier, I saw for a split second that you were sad. It was like a cloak of sadness was covering you, but then it was gone so quickly that I wanted to check with you."

Tina's vision blurred. A cloak of sadness. Those were the exact words that she'd used with God to explain how she felt. A dam burst within and she shook her head. "I'm not okay. That's exactly how I feel. It's like I'm covered by a cloak of sadness, and I don't know why."

Leonie held out her arms and Tina fell into them, desperately trying to wipe away tears that wouldn't stop.

———

TINA CLENCHED HER FISTS AND OPENED THEM AGAIN TO EASE THE nerves that were making them tremble. "Honey? Can I talk to you? It's really important."

Andy muted the TV and made room for her on the couch.

She breathed in deeply, unable to look up. Now that it was time to tell him, she couldn't get the words past the lump in her throat.

Andy ducked his head to see her face better. "What's wrong? Have I done something?"

She shook her head, frustrated with herself that she couldn't speak. Tears spilled down her cheeks.

"Hey." Andy brought her close to him and tucked her into his chest.

She gasped a breath. Why was it so hard to talk about how she felt? "I need to tell you about something that I've hidden from you for a while." The words fell out of her mouth in one big rush.

"What?" Andy asked, suddenly cautious.

"I've been struggling with this 'sadness' ever since Lachie was born. I think I have post-natal depression." She tilted her head to meet his eyes.

He pulled her close again. "I'm not doing well either."

No, he wasn't. "I know."

"I'd rather you get help first. Do you want to see a psychologist?"

"I don't know. I've been journaling with God, and it's helping. If I don't continue getting better though, I'll see a counsellor or something." She sucked in more air and confessed. "I need to get this sorted before the baby comes. I'm really scared that if I have another baby in this state of mind... I don't know what I'll do."

"I'm here for you, whatever you need."

"But you need help too."

"I can wait. I want you to get better."

Then she would have a clearer headspace to help him. "Okay."

4

June 2009

Tina smoothed her hand over her baby bump and struggled to resist the chocolate craving. Argh. Not eating chocolate was hard, but it was best for the new life growing inside. The last doctor's appointment revealed the baby had an irregular heartbeat, and the caffeine in the chocolate she'd been inhaling was the culprit.

She shifted in her seat, glancing over to make sure Lachie was occupied with his breakfast before opening her journal.

Dear Lord,

She paused, unsure of what to write next.
Tell me how you feel.

I'm not sure what I'm feeling.

Start with identifying the emotion.

I know I'm not sad anymore. Since You taught me to prioritise looking after myself, I'm feeling a lot happier. I think the reason I was so sad was because I was mourning myself. In becoming a mother, I lost 'Tina'. Now that I've been rediscovering myself, those feelings have disappeared.

...I'm scared.

Why are you scared?

I'm scared that I won't love this baby as much as Lachie. I don't know how I can fit any more love in my heart... I don't want to be one of those parents that has a favourite child.

...I'm terrified that I'll get depressed.

Visions of not coping with a toddler and a newborn threatened to overwhelm.

I can't go through that again.

ANDY TIPPED UP THE BOTTLE OF WHISKY TO GET THE LAST OF IT out of the bottle. The tumbler was filled half-way. Hopefully it would be enough.

He fell back onto the couch and raised the glass to his lips. The empty wine bottle needed to go in the recycling with the whisky bottle. He'd do that before joining Tina in bed so she didn't find it in the morning.

Heaviness weighed down his eyelids.

His heart raced and he jerked himself awake. Not yet. He couldn't fall asleep. He hadn't drunk enough. The late-night show was boring, so he changed the channel to an English Premier League game.

The game had finished by the time he polished off the whisky and he stumbled through the house getting rid of the evidence before falling into bed.

He spooned behind Tina, her pregnant belly supported by pillows. She shifted in her sleep and murmured something incomprehensible. The pull of sleep dragged him under.

The sound hit him first. Wailing of the bagpipe drones. Sobbing soldiers mourning their fallen comrades. Andy's fingers covered the holes on the instrument as the notes of Amazing Grace filled the atmosphere.

He took a deep breath, blew up the bag and squeezed with his arm to carry the tune to the rows upon rows of soldiers honouring the precession.

He glanced at Commanders, Corporals, Sergeants and Officers. Tears streamed down their faces while the caskets preceded in front of him. Devastation welled up within and he squashed it. This wasn't about him. It was about Meggsy.

The Canadian soldier Andy had befriended in the mess. Critcho's doppleganger. First tour. First time off base. Home in a box. Loud sobs echoed in his mind. Meggsy's mates. Their shoulders shook with the restraint to stand in formation, their battle now one of loss.

This was why he played his pipes for them. To help others mourn the loss of their friend. And his.

The nightmare morphed and with it came gruesome images. Visions of an open casket. Body parts strewn about and blood covered everything.

ANDY JERKED AWAKE. EARS POUNDING WITH HIS RACING HEART, HE struggled for breath. The blankets pooled at his waist; the air cooling the sweat covering his body. He cradled his head in his hands, fingers digging in as if trying to remove the visions. Shoulders heaved with soundless sobs.

He pushed himself off the bed and staggered to his feet. The numbers of the alarm clock blurred. He blinked. Again. Nope. Scrubbing his face, he squinted at the clock. 4am.

Not even a loud thunderstorm would wake Tina, so Andy turned the shower on hot and stepped under the spray. He held his head under the water and braced himself on the cold tiles. His head throbbed with the beginnings of another hangover.

Flashes of his nightmare had him cursing. Would the night time torment stop? Alcohol wasn't working, the bad dreams still came.

He turned off the shower and grabbed his towel. He tried to get his sluggish brain to think. It was Saturday. His breath rushed out. At least he didn't have to front up to work with a raging hangover. His hand grazed over the carpet searching for his sweatpants. Dressed, he ambled to the lounge and turned on the TV.

He didn't realise he dozed off again until Lachie woke up talking in his bedroom. Andy stayed on the couch when his son came through, already dressed for the day and talking to him in his own language.

Tina walked through the open hallway to have a shower.

Lachie looked up at him, his blue eyes earnest and fists already holding a train. He didn't understand what his son was saying. His head still throbbed even after paracetamol, so he nodded and agreed with everything Lachie said.

Tina burst out laughing. "You have no idea what you just agreed to, do you?"

He scratched his head. "Nope."

Her grin grew even bigger. "He asked if you wanted to play trains with him." She paused, a giggle escaping. Argh. His energy plummeted further. "And you just agreed."

He sent a pathetic expression her way, hopeful she would rescue him.

She snickered, raised her hands and stepped back. "Hey, you agreed without finding out what he was saying."

Lachie's pleading eyes pinned him, and he didn't have the

heart to say no. He never could. A part of him knew that it wasn't healthy enough to give his son everything he wanted. The guilt swamped him and he said yes, anyway. He couldn't bear to see Lachie upset. He'd already abandoned him twice in his young life.

His head raged, but he crawled down on the floor and sat back while Lachie connected the train track together. Impressed Lachie had the dexterity and the ability to perceive how to connect the train track ends, Andy noticed that it rarely looked the same twice.

He tried to understand what his son was saying: *garble, garble, garble, Thomas. Garble, garble, garble, James.* When Lachie thrust a red train into his hands, Andy assumed that was James, since Lachie clung to Thomas. More trains appeared with carriages and blocks for buildings.

Being present was tough. The monotony of the trains circling the track reflected his life —going around in circles with no end in sight, except instead of a happy blue train, it was a nightmare that never ended.

August, 2009

TINA STARED DOWN AT THE MINUTES-OLD NEWBORN IN HER ARMS. She should be feeling something but a thick fog enveloped her.

She trembled violently with cold, and it was all she could do to hold onto the baby.

Where was the doctor?

Or Nurse?

Andy?

The fog made it impossible to come up with reasons why she was alone.

Not alone.

The baby. She had to remember the baby.

Her arms cradled the infant, locked in place and paralysed.

Screams had reddened his tiny features but she barely heard them. Her mind struggled to understand. There was so much black hair, a good inch already.

He'd come from her. She knew that much.

Underneath the fog a panic grew. She had no feelings for him. It was love at first sight with Lachie. This son had arrived so quickly at the end, she didn't know what to think.

Couldn't think. Her fears of not loving this baby loomed in her mind.

It felt like she was watching herself from the outside. The baby cradled in her arms, a hundred miles away.

What if she couldn't love him? Fear tightened its grip on her soul.

Andy came back into the room and her mind clung to his appearance. He spoke, but she couldn't understand the words.

She shivered again. "Bl-l-lanket." Her voice croaked.

Andy got up from his chair next to the bed. "What's that?"

She fought to clear the fog. "A blanket, please."

A part of her mind registered he'd gone looking for one, but it seemed like she blinked and her was putting it over her and the baby wailing in her arms.

The warmth settled the chills and clarity seeped slowly back in.

Detached, she studied the baby. He was crying his little heart out. She should do something about that. She was his mother. Her arms loosened from their paralysis and she gently rocked him.

Perhaps he needed to feed. As she fumbled trying to line up her nipple with the baby's mouth, the crying subsided. More clarity returned as she focused on the task.

How long had her son been crying for? The clock in the labour room was opposite her bed. Almost five-thirty.

Tina managed a half-smile at Andy. "What time was he born?"

"4.55pm." He'd been crying for half an hour. What was wrong

with her? Why didn't she feel that same love at first sight this time? Had the post-natal depression caused it?

Shock.

She vaguely remembered first aid courses describing it.

Her shoulders slumped and relief eased her soul. She hadn't expected him to come out after only three pushes. Lachie had to be sucked out after ninety minutes of pushing.

Whatever was wrong with her, it wasn't this little guy's fault. She caressed his swollen little cheek and studied every bit of his face. Instinct took over. She needed to see him.

Tina carefully unwrapped the blanket around him. He startled awake at the cool air.

"Just quickly," she soothed him, "I just want to look at you." She examined the tiny fingers and each little toe before tucking the blanket back around him and latching him back onto her breast. The first tendrils of love made their way past the surreal feeling, crashing through her fears. All at once, maternal love stretched and grew her capacity for love.

Oh. Lord, I get it now. Love isn't divided, it's multiplied. My heart grows bigger to hold the love. She sank into the bed, relief easing her tense muscles.

She tore her eyes from the little bundle in her arms to meet her husband's tired ones. "Where are the nurses?"

Andy shook his head in disbelief. "There's five other women in labour at the moment, and they all have your doctor as their specialist. You were the first to deliver."

Oh. Screams and moans floated down the hallway and she winced. The memory of her own labour brought waves of empathy. "Wow. Six of his patients delivering at the same time, no wonder there's no one here."

As she spoke the words, a nurse bustled into the room. "It's a full house. Let's get you settled into your own room."

Tina waited until she was set in her new private room before asking the nurse, "Can I have a shower?"

"Go right ahead. The bathroom's just off to the side there." She smiled pleasantly and pointed in the direction.

She stroked his cheek as her son continued to suckle. "So," she huffed out a laugh and glanced over at Andy. "A boy. We don't have a boy's name." They hadn't been able to agree.

Andy grinned back, albeit tiredly. "Nope. Do you have any ideas?"

July 2012

IT TOOK ALL OF ANDY'S FOCUS TO KEEP THE NIGHTMARE FROM tormenting his day. Bullet wounds and blown apart bodies tried to parade in his mind.

Tina flounced into the room and did a little spin, but it barely caught Andy's attention. He stretched out further on the couch and stared at the TV screen. If she asked, would he even be able to tell her what was on? He mentally shrugged. He didn't care.

Lachie and his little brother, Callum, were playing in the lounge room. Piles of clothes and bags lay in a corner near the front door. He hated seeing the mess. It drove him crazy. What did Tina do all day?

She drew closer and he caught her just in time as she bounded into him.

"Have you noticed?" She asked.

Huh? "Notice what?" His gaze raked over her, anxious to figure it out before he got in trouble. Her hair?

She pushed off him and twirled again, motioning down her body. "How much weight I've lost."

His breath escaped in a rush as she landed on him again. Not that she was heavy, far from it. He nodded, she had lost a lot of weight. Thanks to the gym membership she'd won, she was the thinnest and healthiest he'd ever seen her. In fact, when he was gone... "You could have any guy you wanted."

Confusion screwed up her face, and she shook her head. "But I don't *want* anyone else." She shrugged, threw her arms around his neck and kissed him.

He grabbed her rear and held her close. While he had the chance.

"Watch me, Mummy." Lachie's high and clear six year-old voice piped up, interrupting the moment. He bounced from cushion to cushion he'd placed on the floor. Callum followed behind trying to keep up. Lachie turned back, jumped and landed on his three year-old brother.

Callum screamed, his little face turning red.

"Tina!" Andy's voice boomed and reverberated around the room.

She'd already rushed over to Callum, checking him over for injuries. Lachie had burst into tears as well and the combined noise had him clenching his fists.

"Just deal with them." He shoved his hands in the direction of the boys.

Tina shot him a dirty look, but he didn't care. Just shut the noise up.

Bribing Lachie and Callum with a treat from the kitchen, Tina hustled them out of the room. At least it was quieter. Kind of.

It lasted about two minutes before they were back in his space yelling and fighting.

"Boys!" He yelled.

Tina hurried into the lounge room and wrapped an arm around each of them. "Daddy's trying to watch his TV show, why don't we go outside and play so Daddy can hear it?"

"Can we go to the park?"

Tina checked her watch, glanced at him and added perkily, "Of course we can. Which one do you want to go to?"

"The one with the boat."

"The boat." Callum parroted.

"The one at the river?" She asked as she gathered their shoes to put on their feet.

"Yeah."

"Alright, Lachie can you please find Callum's sippy cup. Last time I saw it was in the family room." Tina sat Callum down in front of her and put on his shoes. Andy sighed, relieved that they were leaving.

They'd need to get used to him not being around.

5

_____

5th October, 2012

The night was already stressing him out and the night was far from over. Tina's brother was getting married tomorrow and Andy couldn't wait for the whole thing to be over. There were too many people in his space.

Tina had invited friends not going to the rehearsal over for dinner. The extra noise and activity were driving him nuts.

Dinner was two roasts with all the trimmings. Tina had been busy all day preparing for the night, and they'd all sat around the extended dining table afterwards while he'd put the boys to bed. The conversation and wine flowed, more into some than others. He hadn't wanted to come back. He'd fallen asleep putting them to bed and he blinked his eyes to help them adjust to the brightness after the dark bedroom.

Tina's friend Louise flung her wine-filled glass around to make her point. She always had a point, or an opinion, and was happy to share it.

Andy dragged his feet as he returned to the group. It had been a couple of years since he'd seen most of them. Nothing like weddings and funerals to bring people together. He banished images that threatened to take over at the thought of funerals.

Louise's husband, Alec, leaned behind his wife. "Andy, it's been years since we caught up, how was your deployment?"

Alec had served in the Navy before leaving to start his own business. Andy nodded once. Alec would understand. "It was hard. So much loss of life."

Louise piped up, "I didn't think we'd lost that many soldiers." She sipped her wine.

Tell that to the families. "We didn't lose as many as the Americans and Canadians, but any loss is too many."

"The whole thing is a big waste of tax-payers money," Louise declared.

Andy's hackles raised. She had no idea what she was talking about. "We do a lot of good over in the Middle East too. Gone are the days of bombing the shit out of a place and then just leaving. These days we help the locals to recover. Engineers are there rebuilding. We're training and up-skilling—"

"We wouldn't have to do that if we didn't go there in the first place," Louise interrupted.

His lips thinned. "Does anyone want a cup of tea?" She needed to sober up. He got up from the table.

Choruses of 'yes please' and 'no thanks' filled the air.

Tina retrieved a piece of paper and pen. "I won't remember what everyone wants." She laughed.

"I'll go put the kettle on and get everything ready," Andy said, escaping to the kitchen.

He didn't realise he had a follower until he heard her voice behind him. "Don't you think the war is a waste of tax-payers money? You were there, you should know."

He swore in his head. *Drop it*, he silently urged Louise, *and go away*. "No, I don't think it's a waste of tax-payers' money. You haven't been there. You don't see the good that we do."

"All that money should be going to our own country, we

should be looking after our own people first. What about our schools? Our hospitals?"

Tina walked in with the drink orders. She pulled up short as she overheard her friend's words. She frowned behind Louise's back and screwed her face up at him in apology. His shoulders eased. "I've got the list of teas and coffees." Tina held it out.

He took it from her. "Thanks."

Tina turned to Louise. "How's the business going?"

A sigh of relief escaped Andy and he focused on the beverages. Tina led Louise back to the table.

Finally. He paused and inhaled deeply before bringing the last of the hot drinks over to the group.

"The war is a waste of tax-payers' money. You have to see that." Louise leaned across the dining table and refilled her wine glass.

He cursed under his breath. Couldn't she shut up? It wasn't a waste. To say that it was a waste meant that all those lives were lost for nothing. And he couldn't believe that. He wouldn't. "I don't agree with you, Louise." He held his hands up. "I don't want to talk about it anymore."

Silence swept around the table at his firm tone. Tina's stricken gaze met his determined one. He *was* being polite?

"The politicians are just after the oil—" Louise began. All he heard was soldiers died for nothing.

He stood up, almost knocking his chair over backwards. "I'm going to have a shower."

He stalked to the bedroom, shut the door and inhaled a shaky breath. His hands trembled as he rubbed his face. Meggsy's life wasn't wasted. He died for something, not nothing. He felt the sob rising in his chest and he pulled his shirt over his head. He shot towards the ensuite and yanked the hot water tap. Clothes pulled at his feet and he thrust his face under the flow to hide the tears raining down his face.

Tina pressed her hands to her flushed cheeks. She was failing as a hostess. Her friend loved to debate while inebriated, and her husband left to shower in the middle of hosting a dinner. What could she do?

The tension in the room eased as Andy strode off and the topic changed, but she only half-listened.

The shower was on the other side of the dining room wall and she heard the flow of water through the pipes. A long while later, she realised the shower was still on. Andy had long showers, but 40 minutes was ridiculous.

She stood up. "I'm just going to check on Andy, make sure he's alright. That shower has been on for ages." As the words left her mouth the water stopped. She shrugged and sat back down.

When half an hour vanished and Andy still hadn't appeared, she got up from the table, prepared to tell him to come out and join everyone.

Tina tapped on the bedroom door to give him notice she was coming in. She pushed open the door and shut it behind her.

The sight she walked in on stole the words from her lips.

Andy was in the walk-in wardrobe, as naked as the day he was born, bent over and rummaging around his shoes.

She leaned towards him, concerned. He'd been out the shower for half an hour and was still naked. Unease crept along her spine.

Something was very wrong. "Honey? Are you okay? What are you looking for?"

Andy straightened and spun around. A troubled yet absent look covered his face. "What?" He looked around. "Wh-where am I?"

Oh Lord, this is worse than I thought. She walked over to him and hugged his ice-cold body. He held on tight.

She pulled back after a minute. "Where are your clothes? You need to get dressed. You're freezing."

"I-I don't know."

"It's okay. You sit on the bed, and I'll get you something to put on." She led him over to the bed and he slumped over it. "What were you doing in the wardrobe? It looked like you were looking for something?"

"I was looking for the cable." Her brow furrowed. There weren't any in the wardrobe.

Her stomach bottomed out. A flashback. He hadn't had one before. He was getting worse.

Andy absently rubbed a hand down his now trackie-covered thigh over and over.

Lord, what do I do? I'm not sure how to help him. I can't send him back out there. He's in no state to talk to people. And I can't stay in here with a house full.

Put a movie on the laptop and tell him to rest in bed. The words were so clear in her mind.

Okay. *I can do that.*

"How about if I put a movie on the laptop for you, and you can just chill out on the bed for a bit. If you feel like coming out later, you can join us again."

Andy nodded. "Okay."

She set up the computer, chose a random light-hearted action flick and got him comfortable in the bed.

"Are you going to be okay? I need to get back out there."

Andy tore his half-vacant eyes off the start of the movie and peered up at her. He nodded.

"Are you sure? I can get rid of everyone…"

He shook his head. "No, I'd rather watch this."

A corner of her mouth twitched up in a sad smile and she nodded back. "Let me know if you need anything." The door shut softly behind her and she paused. Inhaling a full breath, she straightened her shoulders and went back towards the dining room.

"Is Andy okay?" Marie asked.

I've never seen him like this. She scrounged up a smile. "He will be, he needs some time to chill out."

The conversation flowed again, although this time mostly around her.

Before too long someone looked at the time and murmurings of everyone leaving almost had Tina collapsing in relief.

The bedroom door cracked open and Andy joined them at the front door. He gave Marie and her husband a hug as they were leaving. When he pulled away from them, she noticed a tear in Andy's eyes. *He needs help. But the timing was terrible.*

Not now, she internally begged, *I can't deal with this right now. I've got too much going on with Michael's wedding. I just need to get through tomorrow and then we'll sort it out.*

She walked Marie and the others to the door.

Tina turned around after seeing them out and her jaw flew open. Louise was still trying to get Andy to agree with her. Tina looked over at Louise's husband, hoping he would stop his wife. He shrugged.

"I told you, Louise, I don't want to talk about it anymore." Andy's gruff voice was resolute as he fled the room. He grabbed some dishes and took them to the kitchen.

Louise was right on his heels.

Tina's feet rooted to the ground as she watched the scene before her.

Andy barrelled back around the corner, a fierce expression darkening his face. Louise still followed right behind, arms motioning as she tried to make the same point yet again.

One look at Andy's face broke through the shock that held her paralysed.

"You need to get her home. It's time to go," Tina said to Alec.

Eyes wide, he nodded and reached for Louise. "Come on, it's time to go."

They all made their way to the front door and Andy held it open. Alec slipped through but lost his hold on Louise as she stopped in the open door right before Andy.

Horror blasted within Tina as Louise started up again.

"That money should go towards our schools and our

hospitals. The war is a waste of tax-payers' money. The bloody politicians—"

Andy got in her face and erupted, "Eff off." He thrust his finger into the night. "Get the eff out of my home." He glared at Alec. "Get her effing out of here. You need to get your effing wife under control. She's not effing welcome in my home ever again."

Alec's eyes widened, he reached in and grabbed Louise who still hadn't stopped talking. She wobbled on her heels as Alec dragged her down the sloped driveway. Still arguing.

Andy slammed the door.

Tina peered up at him, her jaw slack.

He looked sternly into Tina's eyes, anger still swirling in his. "She's not to come here."

Tina nodded, horrified.

"If she comes here again… I'm worried I couldn't stop myself."

The implication hung heavy in the atmosphere, and her vision grew watery. She pulled him in for a hug. "I'm sorry. I can't believe that happened."

He squeezed her before pulling away and headed for the kitchen to clean up.

Tina watched him go. What were they going to do when they saw her tomorrow at the wedding?

Tina helped Callum get out of his car seat. He quickly shoved past her to run around the small parking area. Her dad had directed them to a space next their car.

Conflicting desires created a well of irritation within. She rarely saw her family. Apart from her brother, they all lived interstate. As much as she wanted to be there for her husband after the previous evening, it was her brother's wedding day. Her chance to spend time with her extended family. Didn't Andy and the boys get enough of her? Louise had gone too far last night, but surely, he could put it aside for a day? Play happy families for

Michael & Lisa's wedding. How many times had she had to pretend that everything was okay? She'd overcome Post Natal Depression.

Andy kept his dark sunglasses on and stood ten metres away from everyone else. Irritation rubbed at her insides. Couldn't he let last night go?

She walked over to her dad and gave him a hug before calling out, "Callum! This is a car park, you can't run around here."

"I've got him," Andy responded quickly, "You do whatever you need to do."

Dad turned to face her, his face frowning with puzzlement and concern at Andy's unusually standoffish behaviour. "Is Andy alright?"

"No, not really. Louise was drunk last night and wouldn't leave him alone with her opinions on the war." She shrugged a shoulder. "We don't have time to deal with it at the moment." And that broke her heart, it raged at her to help him. But the timing sucked.

Dad walked over and held his hand out to Andy. "How are you going?"

Andy cleared his throat. "Not bad, thanks." His bottom lip wavered and the sight of it speared her chest.

Mum motioned them over to the hotel room. "Have you got Callum's outfit, Tina? Lisa left Lachie's page boy outfit with me."

Tina turned away from the men and held up a cute little suit bag. "Right here."

"I'll just wait out here." Andy jerked his head backwards.

Before long the boys were dressed and ready to go.

Tina smiled at Lachie and Callum, both adorable in their outfits. Lachie, as a page boy, was wearing a miniature three-piece suit complete with special black 'page boy' socks. Callum jumped about in his black trousers, a white collared shirt and a little black waistcoat.

She glanced at the clock on the wall. "Oh. We've still got another forty-five minutes before the ceremony." Attempting to keep dirt off their suits wasn't going to go well. Although, it wasn't Lachie she was worried about. Her little darlin' hated getting dirty. Callum was another story. He was already trying to jump off the bed.

She clapped her hands. "Okay, you two, let's get out of here so Nanny can finish getting ready. You coming, Pop?"

"Nah, you go on ahead, I want to finish getting the camera sorted."

She grinned at her dad's love of gadgets.

Tina caught Callum as he launched off the bed towards the cushion he'd placed on the floor. Or in his imagination, it was no doubt a rock surrounded by molten lava.

"Come on, mischief, let's go and find your daddy."

"Daddy!" Callum wiggled in her arms until she put him down.

He raced over to where the ceremony was prepared on the grass, but his little legs were no match for his older brother. A few people milled around talking while waiting for the service, and a stream of people were walking up the path from the front car park.

As the area filled up, Andy moved further and further away. The boys chased each other in circles around him.

"Honey, we need to find our seats, it'll be starting very soon." She waved her hand to Andy, motioning for them to come closer.

Andy cleared his throat and his shook his head. "Nah, it's alright, I'll stay back here with the boys."

She frowned. "I'd like us all to be together." She waved the order of service booklet. "I need to do a reading, so I have to sit close to get to the microphone."

Andy rubbed his face, but she couldn't see his eyes for the dark sunglasses masking them. His eyebrows furrowed so ferociously that her own irritation sparked again. "No. I'm going to stay back here with Callum. He won't sit still for the ceremony." He gestured to Lachie. "Where does he need to be?"

"I'm not sure, I'll find out." She waved Lachie to her and searched for the groom. Michael told them what he and Lisa wanted Lachie to do and where to stand. Her brother handed over the ring pillow with the fake rings attached. Just in case he lost the real ones.

Her shoulders eased, it was one less thing to stress about.

"You're right to do the reading?" Michael's nerves were beginning to show.

She nodded enthusiastically. "Yep. No worries."

"The celebrant will give you the microphone, you need to make sure that you hold it—"

She smiled. "Michael, I know how to use a microphone. It'll be fine." She leaned in and gave him a quick hug. "You look amazing, I'm so happy for you, Lisa's lovely."

He glanced over to where he expected Lisa to appear. "She's ready. I can see her dad. Take Lachie down there, he'll walk up the aisle after Chloe."

Tina gave Lachie the small pillow with two rings tied to it. "Be careful with this. It's very special." Together they walked over to where a small group had formed waiting for the bride.

The music began and the large group stopped talking as one and turned to face the bride.

Tina fixed a smile on her face and tried not to notice that her husband, instead of standing at her side, was almost fifty metres away. Alone. His fierce expression, bald head and mob-like appearance made sure no one approached.

He wanted this, Andy reminded himself. One last day with his family.

He rubbed away the tear that fell before Tina noticed it. He'd struggled to keep it together throughout the morning, tears had flowed from his eyes without warning, so he kept his distance from people. He didn't want questions. He needed to get through the day.

The bridal party were having their photo session, and Tina wanted one of their own in a secluded little garden.

"Callum. Can you stand next to Lachie, please, pumpkin?" Tina asked. She raised the camera to her eye again at the same time Callum moved away.

He tried to find a smile. "Here, I'll take the photo, you just focus on getting him where you want him." He took photos and even managed a huff of laughter at Tina's ridiculous poses. Lachie and Callum were cute with their suits and 007-style posing.

He gave her back the camera to put away. "That's enough. Let them play." He soaked in playful sounds as the boys climbed and walked on the rock wall. They deserved a better father.

Tina's arms circled around his waist and her head rested on his back. He swallowed the lump in his throat. She deserved more than him. He pulled her around so that she cuddled into his chest.

She squeezed him tight. "Half the day done." Her breath left her in a sudden exhale. "Just the reception to go."

He checked his watch over her head. Only a few hours to go.

———

THE BRIEF REPRIEVE FOR THEIR LITTLE FAMILY HADN'T LASTED LONG enough for Tina. Andy had held her in his arms like he didn't want to let go. He'd embraced her more lately, when for so long he'd barely even touched her. It was like rain after the drought for her soul.

The boys had run around all afternoon and now were exhausted as the speeches went on. She hadn't thought to bring them any food either.

Lachie leaned in close to her "Mum, I'm hungry."

She caressed his hair and whispered, "I know, Sweetheart, I'm sorry. I forgot to bring you some food."

Andy reached for the bowl of dinner rolls. "Here, Lachie, you can have mine."

Callum wasn't to be left out and reached out his chubby little hand.

Tina smiled gratefully at Andy. "Thanks."

He didn't smile back, but nodded and tilted his head back down towards the tablecloth. It had been his position since they'd found their table. He didn't need to tell anyone not to disturb him. The posture and sunglasses he still wore in the darkened function room broadcast it to the entire crowd. He'd sat between the boys as if they were two unexpected sentries or guardians. The wedding was nearly over and then she'd have the focus for the help he needed.

The speeches soon drew to a close and the meals for the children came out first. Michael and Lisa had arranged them for their nieces and nephews.

Conversations circled around her since her focus was on Andy. He didn't even attempt to talk to her parents. Her earlier irritation had morphed into annoyance at his continued anti-social behaviour. What was his problem? Last night sucked. But he didn't need to hold onto it, or take drunk ramblings so personally. *How hard was it to pretend like you actually wanted to be there?* Her brother was only going to get married once. Hopefully. *No, once,* she smiled to herself. Lisa was a gem, and Michael would be insane to let her go. He was crazy, yes, in her 'little sister' opinion, but he wasn't insane.

Andy pushed the boys' half-eaten plates towards the middle of the table. "The boys are finished. I might take them home now and get them into bed."

Tina put down her own cutlery and wiped her mouth with her napkin, just as the DJ announced the beginning of the dancing. "Let them stay. Callum loves to dance."

Andy shook his head. "Nah, it's been a long day. It's already past their bedtime."

She snapped. "Yeah, and it's my brother's wedding. It's okay that they stay up later occasionally." Irritation laced her tone. "They also need to learn resilience." She gestured to Callum already off his chair and bopping to the beat. She exhaled and let the annoyance go with the rush of air. "Let them stay and dance. Callum needs to burn off the lemonade, anyway."

Andy nodded and hunched back over.

The bride and groom did their wedding dance, close family members and the bridal party were up next, and finally she drew Callum onto the dance floor. Her mum and dad danced over to them, bright smiles on their faces. Her parents loved to dance. It was no surprise she and one her sons had inherited the trait too. They danced for a while before Callum's energy faded.

She brought him over to the table where Lachie sat in Andy's lap. "Callum's ready to go home now."

"Okay." Andy set Lachie back onto his own feet and reached under the table for the boys' backpack of spare clothes and other random items. Throwing it over his shoulder, Andy picked up Callum and drew her in for a hug. "Have a good time, stay out as long as you want and enjoy yourself. How are you going to get home since I've got the car?"

"No worries. Dad said I can take his car home and we'll take it back to him after lunch tomorrow." She leaned in to kiss Callum's chubby cheek. "Night, night, sweetheart. I love you."

His heavy eyes looked back at her in love.

"When are you coming home?" Lachie tugged on her hand and she knelt down to his level.

"I'll be home later. You'll already be asleep when I get home, so Daddy is going to snuggle and put you to bed, okay?" It was a habit Andy had begun at bedtime. She hated that the boys relied on him to go to sleep, but she couldn't begrudge the only affectionate time they had with their father.

Lachie nodded.

She brought him close for a cuddle. "Night, night, my darlin'."

"Night, Mummy."

Tina stood up. "See ya, hon." She hugged her husband close. Tomorrow. She'd help him tomorrow.

Andy took off his sunglasses and hugged her tight. He cleared his throat. "See ya. I love you. Have fun."

"I will. Love you too."

"Drive safe." He turned to leave, one son cradled in his arms and the other holding onto his hand.

"You too."

She watched them disappear into the crowd and released a sigh of relief. She rolled her shoulders turned back to the dance floor. It was time to party and start enjoying her brother's special day.

ANDY SNUGGLED ONCE LAST TIME INTO CALLUM'S SIDE. THEY'D read stories in Lachie's bunk and then he'd moved Callum to his bottom bunk and climbed in beside him. They were both asleep. Yet still he lay there. Unable to pull away.

He was glad it was finally over. It had been pure torture to stand amongst so many people. He felt as if everyone could see him barely holding onto his sanity. He'd wiped away countless tears, and stood so far away from everyone so they wouldn't see them rolling down his face.

Looking at the crowd, he'd seen he didn't belong. He didn't deserve to be there. He'd been on the brink of breakdown the entire day. It confirmed his thoughts. He wasn't going to get better. What purpose could he possibly have?

The long day gave him plenty of time to think.

He had plans.

It was time.

He climbed out of the lower bunk without waking Callum and strode through to the kitchen. The medicine box was in the cupboard above the fridge. He painstakingly emptied out the new box of a hundred paracetamol, the new box of ibuprofen, antihistamines, other random tablets, and put them in a snap lock bag. It looked to be about two hundred. He took his whisky glass out of the cupboard and headed to the lounge room.

The litre bottle of whisky Tina had surprised him with last week would wash down the tablets. Between the various pharmaceuticals and a litre of hard spirits, he should go to sleep and not wake up. He gripped the neck of the bottle and took it to the lounge suite.

Andy pulled several small pills from the bag and cradled them in his hands. He wasn't worth the breath in his body.

The family photo frames on the entertainment unit caught his eye and he mentally said his farewells to his boys. They would do better in life if he wasn't there. They would have a new father, he was sure of it. A better one.

He flicked his gaze over to his wedding photo on the wall and thought of his beautiful wife. She'd looked so lovely today, she wasn't going to have any problems replacing him. A better husband was what she needed. The husband she deserved.

Andy unscrewed the whisky bottle. He tipped the tablets into his mouth and his nose wrinkled at the flavour.

He brought the bottle to his lips, but before he could take a sip he heard Tina's voice in his head. Loud. Like the Safety Ranger on a firing range yelling STOP STOP STOP.

Jesus loves everyone. He loves you. You are worthy. He spat out the tablets and wiped his tongue. What the heck?

You are worthy. Jesus can save.

Andy thought about it. What if God was real? Whatever marginal faith he'd had was destroyed in the Middle East. How could God allow it to happen? He clutched the bag of pills.

But what if? He hadn't tried that option. It's not like he had anything to lose.

Andy mentally shrugged and set the implements of his death down. He got on his knees and began talking to the ceiling. "God, I don't know if You can hear me. I don't even know if You're real like my wife says You are, but I want you to save me. If you do, I promise that I will do whatever You want for the rest of my life." He pointed up to where he imagined God to be. "I give you twenty-four hours to do it, or I'll know that You aren't real and I'll just do this again tomorrow night."

Andy sat back on his heels feeling a little stupid. *I can always do it tomorrow.* He got off the floor and tucked the zip-lock bag in the hidden compartment behind the couch. He turned on the TV and poured a glass of whisky. It would give him the courage he needed to go to sleep and face the nightmares.

Only one more night.

6

"Mu-um," Lachie called out too early the next morning. Uhmuh. It wasn't time to get up yet, surely. Although Tina hadn't stayed late at the reception, she'd been home just in time before turning into a pumpkin. She inhaled a deep breath, rolled onto her back and called out, "I'm coming." She flopped out of the bed, feet crashing on the carpet and went to see what she was needed for.

"I'm hungry." Of course, he was. She looked forward to the days when the boys were able to get their own breakfast.

After getting them their toast, she returned to her bedroom. Andy lay unmoving underneath the covers. He'd already been asleep by the time she'd made it home last night. And still he slept, with no signs of getting up.

She headed to the ensuite and stepped into the foggy warmth of the shower.

Hmmm… Sunday today. Church. Nope. Not today. Andy needed her. She couldn't help him yesterday.

Today, he had her focus. Guilt crashed over her for not giving him her attention yesterday. She'd rationalised and justified that Andy had stopped them from going to so many family functions, and she refused to let him miss her brother's wedding. But had it been the right choice?

Go to church, a quiet voice urged in her spirit.

What? No. She'd already decided. Tina turned off the water and towel-dried. On her way past the bed to the walk-in wardrobe, she gently asked Andy, who was blinking sleep out of his eyes, "Are you getting up anytime soon?"

He shook his head, silently begging for understanding before burying it back under the covers. "I can't."

This was worse than she'd thought. She nodded once. Her voice gentled further, "Okay. You stay in bed if you need to."

A stray thought crossed her mind. "Will you be able to go to work tomorrow?"

Andy peered over the edge of the blanket. "Yeah. I feel safe at work." Pain blossomed at the implication that home didn't feel safe.

Go to church, the voice urged, more insistent this time.

No! I won't abandon him. It was bad enough that I didn't do anything yesterday. He needs me.

You need to go to church.

Why?

Go.

She grumbled back to the voice, *Fine. I'll go. There better be something at church that I needed to hear.* And it better be important.

"I'll take the boys to church and give you some peace and quiet. Don't forget I need to take Dad's car back to him later."

"Okay." The blankets muffled Andy's voice.

She stalked out of the room. "Come on, boys, let's get you dressed and ready for church."

Tina sat with her arms folded across her chest during the 10am Anglican service. There'd been nothing in the songs they'd sung that 'spoke' to her. Nothing in the sermon. It was a good message, but there was no Vegas-lit signs from God that would account for why she had to be there that morning. The priest gave the final benediction.

She raised her eyes to the ceiling, *Well, that was a waste of time,* she told Him. Releasing her arms, she sighed. She may as well stay for the morning tea. There had been a new face that she hadn't seen before and she liked to welcome new people.

After getting a mug of tea and a biscuit, she made her way to the stranger. "Hi, I'm Tina," She stretched out her free hand.

"Peter." He met her hand with his and shook.

She smiled as she released him. "I haven't seen you around before, is this your first time here, Peter?" She said his name again, hopeful that she'd remember it.

"Yeah." He bobbed his head.

"If you don't mind me asking, what brought you here today?" Curiosity infused her tone.

"I'm in the Army and I'm just stopping in on my way through. I've got travel further north to Queensland."

"Oh! My husband used to be in the Army. He's RAAF now, but he used to be infantry. What do you do in the Army?"

He hesitated, as bracing himself for an unwanted response. "I'm a psychologist."

Get out. A sudden quickening in her spirit told her exactly why she had to be at church today. Tears pricked her eyes and she blinked them back. She peered up into his face. "I really need to talk to you." She added thickly, "It's about my husband."

He examined her face. "Sure, is there somewhere we could go for privacy?"

She nodded and led him out of the room. Father David, who preferred to be addressed by his first name, passed them in the hall. "David, do you mind if Peter and I speak privately in the library? I need to talk to him." She knew it was an odd request, but she silently begged him.

David tilted his head curiously. "That's fine."

Tina showed Peter the library and sat down at the table. Peter shut the door behind him. She sat up in surprise. "You don't need to shut the door."

He shrugged. "If we're going to talk in a professional capacity, I'd prefer that you have the privacy."

Tina shrugged a shoulder in agreement.

Peter took a seat opposite. "What did you want to talk about?"

She blurted out, "I think my husband has PTSD."

He nodded in compassion, "Is he functioning or non-functioning?"

"What does that mean?"

"Functioning means he can still go about everyday life, and non-functioning means that he can't function in everyday life."

She took a shaky breath. "He used to be functioning, but an incident happened on Friday night with a family member and now he's non-functioning. He said he couldn't get out of bed this morning."

"Has he been diagnosed?"

"This is the first time I've told anyone what I think is happening. I don't think he was ready to get help. But now he's not…"

"Is he able to go to work tomorrow, do you think?"

"Yeah, he told me before that work is a safe place for him. He'll be able to turn up tomorrow."

He nodded. "And you want to get him help, or for you?"

The question confused her. Why would she need help? She was fine, Andy wasn't. "I want help for him."

"Okay. This is what we can do. I've just come from Singleton Army Barracks. I don't work there anymore, but I do know some people that can help," Alex listed off four options of places and people Andy could talk to.

None of them gave her peace in her spirit. "Okay…"

He must have seen her hesitation. His face lit up. "There's another person that would be ideal, her name is Alice."

That one, she felt the wordless certainty.

"Yes. Alice." Her confidence rang in her voice, "Can you tell me more about her?"

"She's a civie, sorry, civilian contractor working at Singleton Barracks and she's worked with a lot of soldiers with PTSD."

"That's perfect. How can I get a hold of her?"

"I'll organise it for your husband. What's his name?"

"Corporal Andrew Summers."

"Do you know his service number?"

She snorted. "Ah, no. I don't remember it." She hardly remembered phone numbers and birthdays.

Peter looked down at the desk and tapped his thumbs together.

"What do you need it for?" She asked, after the silence grew awkward.

He glanced back up at her. "I need his service number to be able to contact him."

"Oh. Can you do a search on the DRN?" Hopefully the Defence network was tri-service.

"Yeah, but it covers the whole of the Defence Force. If there is ten Andrew Summers' I won't know which one to contact."

Excitement bubbled, tickling her soul, "There's only two Andrew Summers' in the service at the moment, and my Andy is the only one posted to Williamtown." She lifted a shoulder. "He told me he sometimes gets the other Andrew's emails."

Peter sat back in his chair. "Great, no worries. I'll look up Andrew first thing in the morning and I'll call him then. Tell him to expect a phone call from a Captain Peter Felix."

Joy, excitement and a gratitude towards God, fought for dominance all the way home. Andy was getting help.

———

ANDY ROLLED OVER IN BED, THE QUIETNESS OF THE HOUSE ECHOED the dangerous emptiness in his soul. There was only one way out of the hell he was in. God wouldn't come through for him. He scoffed, that's if He was even real, or that He cared.

He rolled back the other way. Now he waited. His last day and he couldn't even get out of bed. He wasn't worth it. He didn't deserve to live.

The blankets suffocated, and he pushed them off to check the time. Noon. Half a day and it was over.

The car pulled up the steep driveway, car doors slammed. Little boy excitement mixed in with a calming feminine voice. They deserved so much better than him. He'll get out of their way.

The front door turned. "Hey honey, we're back."

"Daddy!" Lachie and Callum leaped onto the bed and he sat up to hug them.

Tina paused in the doorway, leaning on the frame. "You will never guess who I met at church this morning."

He wasn't in the mood for games. "Who?"

"An Army psychologist."

He stilled. What the? "You're kidding."

She shook her head, sending her ponytail flopping. "Nope." A beaming smile overtook her face. "He was just visiting, said he was on his way up to Queensland."

Andy's jaw went slack.

She continued, oblivious his entire world had just been rocked. "He'll look you up on the DRN first thing tomorrow morning, and he'll talk to you about options then. He gave me some…"

It was too much for his brain and he tuned her out. He'd challenged God last night to save him, not even believing He was real. This morning, Tina connected with an Army psychologist who happened to be at her church that day. He would get the help he needed.

The coincidence was too much. He stumbled to his feet, legs tangling in the covers in his haste. He grabbed Tina's forearm. "God is real."

Tina frowned at him, confusion contorting her face. She nodded slowly. "Yeah. I know God is real."

She didn't get it. This was huge. God was real. He'd shown Himself in less than the twenty-four hours.

Tina turned around, calling out over her shoulder, "I'm going to put the kettle on, do you want a cuppa?"

He nodded, distracted. It wasn't until she turned back in question that he realised he hadn't answered her out loud. "Sure."

The boys tore out of the room after her and Andy collapsed to his knees. *You're real. Tina said you were, but...* He remembered his promise from the night before. *From now on, I will do whatever You want me to do, because I'm a man of my word.*

———————

ANDY GOT READY FOR WORK AS USUAL THE NEXT DAY. HE ALWAYS got to work fifteen minutes early thanks to the work ethic instilled in him by his father.

"You seem to be better today." Tina tilted her head sideways, a small smile curving her lips.

He grabbed his ID and wallet. "That's because work is a safe place." How many times did he have to say it?

"I wasn't sure since you were barely functioning all weekend." She headed for the walk-in robe, tripping on her clothes strewn about the floor.

The mess drove him nuts. "If you cleaned up your clothes, you wouldn't trip over them."

"Yeah, well, you knew what I was like when you married me." Her pert tone matched her hand on her hip.

Andy drummed his ID on the tallboy. He needed to tell his Sergeant about Saturday night and his aborted suicide attempt. Confessing was like opening up hastily laid bandages over a wound. Bare, raw and bleeding.

Dressed in jeans and a t-shirt, Tina flung her arms around his neck. His fingers hooked in her belt loops and pulled her close. He couldn't tell her what he'd nearly done. He hung his head and buried it in the crook between her neck and shoulder.

Seconds counted down in his mind, but he didn't want to leave yet. To face it. He inhaled deeply, her fruity shower-gel fragrance filling his nostrils, before releasing his hold. "I've got to go. You said Captain Felix was going to call at 7am?"

She pulled back and pecked him on the lips. "Yeah. He'll probably tell you your options. Alice seems to be the best choice, but go with what you want."

"Okay."

"Let me know how you go." Tina headed to the lounge room where Lachie and Callum sat transfixed to ABC Kids. "Lachie, do you want me to help you get ready for school?"

When Andy arrived at work, the building was bustling as more and more people arrived.

He swiped his ID over the security panel and punched in the code to his workspace.

Sergeant Bass sat behind his desk and Andy released a long, drawn out breath. Clenching his fingers to stop the tremble. Beelining straight for his boss, he shut the door behind him and blurted, "I attempted suicide on the weekend."

Bass jerked to his feet. "You did what?" His eyes huge in his face. "Stay here. I'll be back." He strode out and dragged Jed, another corporal into the office. Bass pointed at them. "Jed, stay here with Summo. I'll be right back."

"Is everything okay?" Jed asked.

He cleared his throat. "I attempted suicide on the weekend." He couldn't meet his eyes.

Shock rippled across Jed's face. A heartbeat passed. He almost lost his footing when his mate yanked him forwards in a hug and didn't let go.

Andy's vision blurred and his chest heaved with a suppressed sob.

The phone rang.

Jed answered it in the workshop, but came through few seconds later. "There's a Captain Felix on the phone for you."

Andy checked the time. 0700. "This is Corporal Summers."

"Hi, Corporal Summers, may I call you Andrew?"

"Sure."

"I spoke with your wife yesterday. She was worried about you, she said that you were no longer functioning in everyday life."

The third time still brought a lump to his throat, but the words escaped the blockage, "I attempted suicide on Saturday night."

"I see. Are you still considering suicide?"

"No. Not anymore."

"Okay. I've posted to Queensland, but I have some contacts that can help you."

Andy listened for a few minutes as the captain named different options and people. None of them really appealed to him.

"Oh. And there's a civie psychologist, Alice." The Captain added, "She's worked with others before like yourself. She's out at Singleton Army Barracks."

That caught his attention. He'd done his infantry training at Singleton Army Barracks. It was home.

"I'd like to see Alice."

———

ANDY WALKED IN THE DOOR AFTER WORK AND SET HIS KEYS, WALLET and ID down on the dresser. He unpacked the rest of his bag.

"Daddy! Daddy!"

Little rockets crashed into his legs and buckled his knees.

He rubbed them both on the head. "Hey, boys."

Tina followed behind and sat on the bed "How was your day?"

He ducked his head, and pretended to be interested in his bag. "Yeah, good."

"How did your first psych appointment go?"

He shrugged. What could he say? He wasn't suddenly better. He felt just as hopeless going in as he did coming out. What the appointment even achieve? "Jed came with me."

"Oh, that's good. I'm glad you weren't by yourself. He waited in the waiting room?"

"Yeah, Alice came out and introduced herself. She seemed glad he came, too. In fact, she suggested that I bring someone every session."

"Is that to keep you company on the way and back?"

"Yeah, she also suggested going out for either lunch or a cuppa before heading back to work to clear my head."

Tina nodded. "That sounds like a good idea. Will you ask Jed?"

"Nah, he can't be away from work that long. I need to go three times a week to start."

She didn't look surprised that he'd be going so often. "Who will you ask to go with you?" She gave a wry smile as she watched Callum playing. He easily followed her thoughts. There was no way she'd be able to come. Not that he wanted her to. He didn't want her to see him so raw and vulnerable.

"Mum! Mum! Mum!" Callum tugged on her arm.

"What, darling?" She turned her attention to their youngest.

Andy rolled his eyes and stormed out of the room. Every. Time. He couldn't even have one conversation with her that the boys didn't interrupt multiple times.

He filled the kettle and set it to boil.

"Sorry, hon." Tina grabbed a mug out for herself. "I've set him up with the TV."

He inhaled his frustration and tried again. "I was thinking of asking Grieve."

Surprise laced her tone, "That's a good idea. I know you've been getting close to him."

"Well, he's the one that comes and checks on me when I run out of church if I have an anxiety attack. He's retired, so hopefully he'll have the time to come with me. I feel safe with him."

Tina's smile grew fond. "Grieve is a great person to ask. I'm sure he will."

"Have we got their phone number?"

"Yeah, it's in the blue address book…. Wherever that is. I'll find it for you."

He nodded and poured the coffee and tea.

"So, what did you talk about with Alice?" Tina reached for her tea but pulled up short. "Oh! You don't have to tell me. I'm just saying, if you want to talk about it, I'm here to listen."

He contemplated the idea. There was stuff that he didn't want her to know. Like the conversation they'd had about his suicide attempt. Shame overwhelmed him. Besides, Alice seemed satisfied he wasn't suicidal. Not that his life was suddenly worth living, but he believed that God had saved his life and he attempt to take it again.

He cast about his memory for something to share. "Alice had me write down on a piece of paper all the good things about myself and all the bad."

"How did you go?"

"I wrote three things that were good."

Her eyebrows shot up, "What did you write?"

He shrugged. "I don't remember." He honestly couldn't.

"What about the bad?"

He met her blue gaze. "I filled an A4-sized sheet, and I could've kept going." Not deserving. Bad husband. Bad father. Worthless…

"Oh, honey." Tina pulled him close for a hug and he gripped her tight. She deserved so much better than him.

He pulled away.

"Did she give you a diagnosis?"

"Yeah, it's Post Traumatic Stress Disorder. She gave me a few options to think about where to go from here. There was one that has the most success rate for simple PTSD."

"What's simple PTSD?"

"I think Alice said it's where the trauma was a solitary incident, or happened over a short period of time. Complex PTSD is when the trauma happens over years."

"What was the option that had the most success?"

He shifted his weight. "It's called 'exposure therapy'. Alice would take me back to the moment of the trauma and talk me through it. They reckon it's the hardest to do because you have to go back and 're-live' the trauma."

Tina nodded in compassion. "That would explain why they don't do it for the Complex PTSD. If they went back to each traumatic event, it would take years."

He nodded, nausea twisting his stomach. "It would be too hard."

"What were the other options?"

He rattled them off, but suspected the way forward for him was going to be the toughest route. "Which one do you think I should do?"

Tina rubbed her hand down his arm. "I'll support you whichever one you choose. But I have a feeling that exposure therapy will be the best one. If it gets the best results, then maybe it's the best option. I don't think you need medication. Do you?"

He wasn't sure. "If I go for the medication, then I have to go to a psychiatrist. I like Alice, I don't want to see someone else."

Tina grabbed a cutting board and knife. "You were functioning okay until the weekend, when suddenly you weren't. Since Sunday, though, you've been functioning again. How about you leave it as a backup?" Tina spoke the last from inside the fridge as she grabbed the ingredients for dinner.

Andy exhaled a long breath. He didn't have a problem taking medication. He'd been on it before when he'd fallen into depression after battling Chronic Fatigue Syndrome. Besides, Alice was going to give him coping mechanisms to deal with the anxiety.

Later that evening, Tina found the address book and gave him Grieve's number. Grieve was compassionate when he told him of his diagnosis. He'd said that he wanted to be the one to support him. Andy told him the day and time of the next appointment and hung up.

He hated to be a burden.

7

C hurch on Sunday was hard. Andy hadn't been since he'd had an anxiety attack during the service, but since he'd promised God to follow Him, he should go back.

He pulled up to the nineteenth century church with trembling hands. The rest of the family piled out of the car. He held the boys' hands to get himself under control.

Sweat beaded on his close-shaven head. "You go on ahead." He motioned to Tina. "I'll let the boys play outside till the service starts." *And my heart rate calms down.*

Five minutes later, he followed, leaving his entrance till the last moment, heading to the newer addition where they held a more contemporary service.

He didn't last very long.

In ten minutes, he left with sweat pouring off him and heart racing. He collapsed on the stone bench around the side of the church and held his head in his hands. His chest heaved with sobs. He was a pitiful excuse for a man. Couldn't even sit through a church service without bolting out.

Movement out the corner of his eye shot his head up. Grieve came around the corner and paused before coming closer. "Are you alright?" he asked, the Scottish heritage clear in the rolling 'r's.

Andy couldn't respond. He buried his face in his hands.

A warm weight settled across his shoulders. Andy pulled his hands away as Grieve sat on the cold bench next to him.

Grieve didn't speak.

Andy's shoulders eased under the comfort of a friend and his heart rate slowed back to normal.

Sometime later, he cleared his throat. "Thanks, Grieve." The words struggled out of his still-tight throat.

Grieve patted his knee. "No worries, mate." He motioned back to the church. "Did you want to go back in?"

His heart seized and he shook his head frantically. "No."

"That's fine. We can just chat out here if you like. Did you watch the soccer last night?"

Andy's lips twisted, ruefully. His team had tanked. "Unfortunately."

Before long the service ended and people began leaving the church grounds. Grieve stood up. "I'll go and let Tina know where you are. She looked concerned when you left."

He focused on the grass. "Sure." His cheeks grew hot. What must Tina have thought of him running out of the service. He was such a coward.

Minutes later, two excited little boys rounded the corner. "Daddy! We found you," they shouted like it was some game.

"Yep. You sure did."

Lachie pointed to a large, open grassed area. "Can we go over there?"

Tina walked around the corner in time to hear the question. "Yes, but don't go over near where the flower garden is. That's a special area."

Irritation swept through him. Churches and their rules. "Why?"

Tina tilted her head sideways, her brow furrowed. "It's the memorial garden and I don't think it's appropriate for the boys to run around in there. That would be disrespectful." The boys ran off and she sat down next to him. "Are you okay? I was going to come out after you when you left, but Grieve waved at me to stay."

He wiped away the sweat that formed at the idea of her seeing him in that state. "No, I'm glad you stayed. If you'd come out the boys would have come too." He neatly dodged her question.

"Warren Handley asked if you were okay, too."

"Who's Warren again?" All the people gelled together in his mind.

"Warren's the Vietnam Vet, and he does stuff for Legacy."

Now he remembered. Warren checked in on him every now and then.

Tina broke through his thoughts. "I hope you don't mind, but I told him about your diagnosis."

He shook his head. "I trust Warren. It's fine."

She rose. "I need to go back inside quickly and speak to someone before we go. Be about five minutes."

He nearly snorted but caught himself just in time. Yeah, right. More like fifteen to twenty minutes. Tina would see someone on her way and chat with them first, and countless others before she came back outside. "I'll stay and watch the boys," he said, casually checking the time.

He got lost in his thoughts keeping one eye on the boys so they didn't run onto the road.

"Andy."

He half-turned to see who had called his name. "Oh. Warren." He stood and extended his hand. "It's good to see you."

Warren put an arm on his shoulder while they gripped hands. "Tina told me you've been diagnosed with PTSD."

They both settled into their own space, and Andy resumed his watch over the boys. "Yeah. I went to see the psych on Wednesday."

"You've made the first step, mate. It's the hardest one to make. I was diagnosed with PTSD a few years ago."

That caught his attention. "Yeah?"

Warren nodded. "There's been a few guys who have been diagnosed now."

Something eased inside at the knowledge he wasn't the only one.

"Do you mind if I give you some advice, Andy?"

He shrugged. "Sure."

"Take Tina to one of your psychologist appointments."

Andy's brows quirked.

"It's really important that she knows what's going on and what your treatment would be like. Meeting with your psychologist and putting a face to a name will put Tina at ease."

Warren would have seen a lot of this with his work with Legacy. They often had dealings with the families of veterans. If he thought it was a good idea, it was. Andy nodded. "I will, thanks Warren."

At that, Tina bustled out of the building and he glanced at his watch. Yep. Twenty minutes.

November, 2012

TINA GAZED OUT THE FRONT WINDSCREEN WHILE ANDY DRUMMED his fingers on the steering wheel.

"What time is your appointment again?"

"11 o'clock."

She glanced at the clock on the dashboard. There was plenty of time. Although Singleton was about an hour away, they'd stopped at a McDonalds on the way since they were still too early after dropping the boys off at school and preschool.

"I know we discussed it earlier, but I don't remember you choosing... have you decided which treatment plan?"

Andy rubbed his hand back and forth on his bald head. "Yeah,

I'm going to go with the exposure therapy. I just want to rip the band-aid off, so to speak. Get it over and done with."

He was so brave. How many other people would choose the easy option instead?

She reached over and rested her hand on his thigh. "You've got this. I know from what you've told me that it's going to be difficult." She couldn't imagine how hard it would be to go back to the traumatic events. She squeezed his leg. "But you're strong and courageous. It's going to take a lot of courage to do this, but I know you can. God will help you too."

He gave what she called the 'yeah, whatever' look. He didn't believe he was brave. She smiled sadly out the window. Maybe one day he would see himself how she saw him.

"Have you got your ID card ready? We're almost there." Andy's voice held a tinge of consternation.

Tina scrambled around in her enormous handbag.

Andy flattened his lips and shook his head. Her lack of organisation often frustrated him. She glared back.

"Well, if you got it ready when we got in the car, this wouldn't happen every time."

Irritation bloomed. *Oh shut up.* That wasn't helping. She saw the gate rapidly approaching and her searching intensified. Her fingers touched the hard corners of the ID and she triumphantly pulled it out.

They pulled up to the front gate of the Army Barracks and held up their identification while the guard at the gate checked them and let them pass.

"You need to keep it visible at all times. They can be strict," Andy warned.

She clipped the ID holder to her shirt.

Andy drove to the base's slow speed limit and pointed out the buildings he knew, where he'd done his training all those years ago. Although there'd been some changes, it was still mostly the same. Minutes later, they pulled into a car space in front of the medical centre.

She didn't quite know how to describe the turmoil that filled her. Nervousness at meeting her husband's psychologist, a little jealous that Alice would know Andy on a deeper level than she did. Her possessive nature wasn't thrilled with that. A sudden peace and confidence overlay her nerves reassuring her everything was going to be okay.

Andy liked Alice, she reassured herself, and we both thought she was the best option. Taking a deep breath, she walked through the doorway of the waiting room. It looked just like a GP's waiting room, except the posters around the room focused on mental health hotlines and information, not skin cancer, vaccinations and the dangers of drinking alcohol during pregnancy.

"Alice's office is in there." Andy pointed to a door and relaxed back into a chair.

Tina nodded her head in surprise. She hadn't expected it to look so normal and comfortable. "Alice knows I'm here today, right?"

"Yeah. She said as long as I was happy with you being in there. We won't be talking about my issues today."

Maybe that's why Andy seemed so comfortable. There was no pressure. "You're certain you want me there?" She motioned her head towards the offices.

"Yeah, it makes sense. That way you know what's going on with me."

A woman around Andy's age opened the door and smiled at Andy. She was dressed in comfortable professional attire, but her loose curly brown hair softened the look. She approached them with her hand extended. "Hi, I'm Alice. You must be Tina."

They grasped hands briefly and Tina returned an easy smile. "Yes, it's nice to meet you."

Alice waved a hand. "Come on through. I'll take you to my office. I've not long changed rooms since we've had a turnover in staff so I'm still getting used to which way to go."

The next hour flew by as Alice first explained Post Traumatic

Stress Disorder to them both. It was a re-wiring of the pathways in the brain due to trauma. She then took them through the different treatment options, describing what would happen. She'd explained exposure therapy with a rough example of someone traumatised by an experience in a lift. The first time perhaps they would get near the lift. Bring their anxiety levels down and leave. The second time, touching the lift button, bringing the anxiety levels down again before leaving. The third time getting in the elevator, but leaving the doors open, and so on. Each time getting further and further towards being able to be in a lift and adjusting anxiety levels using grounding and breathing techniques.

Since Andy's situation wasn't one he could go back to physically, Alice would get him to close his eyes and mentally take him back to the Ramp Ceremonies, talking him through grounding and breathing techniques. It was going to be recorded on his phone so he could replay it during the week for homework. He'd need a quiet place where he felt safe.

Because the sessions were tough, Alice wanted Andy to make sure he had some company before and after the session. Not going straight back to work after talking about some difficult topics, but having space to unwind and breathe before getting back to everyday life.

The sessions were going to be difficult, and take a toll of Andy mentally and emotionally. Alice advised Tina to not expect too much from him on those days. She encouraged Andy to communicate his capabilities to Tina on the days that he was struggling so she'd adjust her expectations and therefore lessen any frustrations.

When they said goodbye in the waiting room, Tina again shook Alice's hand. "Thank you for letting me crash the session today."

Alice smiled back and nodded her head towards Andy. "Thank Andy. It was his idea. Today's discussion was what treatment option Andy wanted to go with."

"She's lovely," Tina commented as they walked out to the car. Her earlier worries seemed ridiculous now. Warren had been right. She felt so much better about it all now she'd met Alice and knew what to expect.

"Yeah, I like Alice. She's not like other psychologists I've met."

"So, what are we going to do now? There's still a couple of hours before we have to go home."

"Remember, Alice wants me to have coffee or lunch before I go back to work. Where do you want to go?"

She considered it. "Morpeth?" The historical town had some lovely coffee shops.

"That's where Grieve suggested."

Her mouth turned down, she wished she could take him every time, but with small kids it wasn't possible. Not wanting to dwell on the negative, she pulled herself up. She was grateful they had Grieve.

———

"DADDY'S HOME!"

Andy tried to push past Lachie and Callum to get inside. "Hi, boys."

"Hi, honey." Tina came through wiping her hands on a tea towel.

He nearly fell over. She'd washed dishes. Who was this woman and where was his wife? "Hi, honey."

"How did your psych appointment go today?"

He ruffled the boys' heads as they followed him into the bedroom and put his bag on the bed to unpack. The psych appointment had been challenging. "It was hard." He cleared his throat and bobbed his head down. The noise from excited little boys reverberated in his skull. It pounded, intensifying the headache he'd had since finishing with Alice earlier in the day. "I'm exhausted. I'm going to have a nap."

"No worries." Tina shoed the boys into the family room.

"Lachie, we still have to do your home reader." She closed the bedroom door and the noises muffled.

He refreshed himself with a shower and fell into bed. He battled stirred up memories from the exposure therapy. Lines of soldiers, airmen and airwomen forming a corridor. His heart spiked and he squeezed his eyes tighter. He didn't want to go back there again.

What did Alice say to do again? He pinched the bridge of his nose. Grounding techniques. Get back in touch with reality. He opened his eyes and focused on naming the furniture in the room. Anything he saw.

Desk.

Chair.

Picture Frame. It had a wooden frame.

Bedside lamp. Square shade. Cream.

His breathing evened out. When had he lost his breath?

Pillow.

Blanket.

Door. Painted cream. Door handle. Circular.

Hands, no longer trembling.

His eyes slowly drifted shut and he slipped into a brief and dreamless sleep.

"HEY, SUMMO," ANDY'S SERGEANT CALLED OUT FROM HIS OFFICE.

Andy stuck his head around the office door. "Yeah, Bass?"

"What time did you want to go and do what you need to do?"

Do what he needed to do? Oh. The homework he had from Alice. They'd made available a small windowless room in the work building to do his exposure therapy homework. Apart from home, work was the only place he felt safe.

He was fortunate his hierarchy were supportive. They gave him the time and space to go to his psych appointments, and the associated homework. "I'll set the part I just finished working on to do a final test. That one will take an hour to complete. If I go during the test, I should be back by the time it finishes."

Bass paused from searching through his papers to meet his gaze. "Don't feel you have to hurry. I get that you need to do it."

He hated putting anyone out, but doing the homework was a necessary part of the therapy. "Sure. Thanks Bass."

Andy headed back out to the workstation and connected the part of the enormous testing machine. He pushed a few buttons and waited until the machine responded.

His hand trembled as he grabbed his phone with the voice recording on it and headed into the allocated room.

The door shut out the outside world.

A chair and table perched next to a wall and he settled in. Nerves squirmed. He hated this.

Pressing play on the phone, the room disappeared as Alice's voice took him back to the Middle East.

The jet fumes stung his nostrils, but he needed breath to blow up the bagpipe bag. He exhaled into the mouthpiece and his arm raised as the bag inflated. The drones hummed in harmony.

He was slow marching behind the caskets. Meggsy's casket. He fought off a wave of tears that threatened to take him under as he continued his slow cadence. The haunting notes of Flowers of the Forest filled the area.

Andy flicked his eyes to the sides, he wanted to make sure he was doing what he could to help Meggsy's mates and countrymen mourn the loss of their friend and workmate. The lights caught the tracks of tears on the faces of the Commanders. He wobbled but pressed on towards Meggsy's mates barely holding themselves together.

Alice's voice still spoke in the back of his mind, asking him to gauge his current anxiety levels on a scale from one to ten. One being completely at peace and ten being as high as anxiety could go.

Sweat had broken out on his forehead. His heart raced. Dry mouth. Shaking.

The door abruptly opened breaking into whatever held him.

"Sorry, man." The voice paused. "Are you alright?"

Andy dragged his arms away from the top of his head and peered up from the floor. His face slack and wet with tears, his body huddled into a tight ball in the corner of the room. He cleared his throat. "Yeah, I'll be okay." He didn't believe it.

The door shut but it was too late, he sat on the floor exposed and vulnerable.

8

_____

March, 2013

Tina reached for her pen and journal. It had become her lifeline.

Dear Lord,

Thank You so much for this beautiful day! Thank You for my family, for Andy, who works hard to support us, even while he's struggling to survive each day.

Thank You for my boys, they light up my life. Parenting is hard, but I'm so glad that You are with me every step of the way. Thank You for the wisdom and guidance You give me when I have no idea what to do.

You have blessed me so much, and I want to be a blessing for other people. You have done so much for me, I want to pass that on.

She put the pen down to take a sip of her tea. A burning desire developed in her chest to help someone, anyone who was truly in need.

Glancing at her watch, Tina lurched forward to put her tea down. They were going to be late!

"Lachie! It's time to go to school!" How he was old enough to be in his second year of primary school was beyond her. Babies grew up too fast.

After dropping Lachie at school, Tina drove another ten minutes to their church for bible study. She turned left and slowed as she approached the front of the building. A 4WD had parked out the front with its hood raised. Someone had their head under it, and two women waited next to him. One raised her arms up and down in a panic.

The burning sensation returned in her chest.

Were these the people she needed to help?

The fire within grew hotter. ***You asked for an opportunity.***

Tina's smile grew wide as she unbuckled Callum's harness. He flung his arms out of the seatbelt and wiggled down. She halted him before he could climb out of the car. Three-year-olds were a handful and a half. "Wait, Callum. I see some people that might need some help. I need you to stay with me and not run into the church just yet."

"Where are they? How do you know?"

She pointed at the car. "You see that car with the front open?"

Callum nodded.

"I think their car broke down and they're stuck. How lucky it happened right outside of our church so we could help them, huh?" She closed the doors and pressed the button to lock the car. "Come on," she said, reaching for his little hand.

"No!" Arrgghh. The one child who most needed to hold hands for his own safety and he hated it. She saved the battle for when it was a necessity.

Raising empowered children sometimes sucked. "Fine, but in that case, you need to stay on the footpath."

"Okay." He ran a few paces ahead of her.

Nerves squirmed in her stomach as she approached the small group. "Hi." Tina waved awkwardly. "I pulled up to come to church, and I noticed that your car's broken down?" She turned it into a question in case she'd misunderstood the situation.

A thin man came out from under the hood, wiping his hands

on his shirt. "Yeah. It was weird. We got to this spot and the car just stopped." He continued to describe what he'd discovered in his investigations, but it meant nothing to Tina.

"I can't really help with that, I have no idea about cars." She splayed her hands in apology. "But I can offer you the use of the phone at the church, or if you need to use the bathroom, you can."

"No. We're fine." One of the women piped up first.

The man leaned in close to her and they discussed quietly amongst themselves.

Tina stood, out of place, while she waited. "Listen, it's okay if you don't want to. I thought you might want some help, that's all," she said, smiling to show she wasn't offended. "Come on, Callum." He ran ahead again as headed back to the church.

"Wait!"

Tina turned back to the group.

"Are you sure it's okay?"

"Of course, it is. It's a church. This is what we do. Help people who need it."

The man spoke up, "I think I know what's wrong. I have to call a place and see if they've got the part I need."

Tina smiled. "Sure. Come on, I'll take you to the phone."

———

THE NEW PRIEST HAD STARTED AT THE CHURCH ONLY A COUPLE OF weeks earlier. Andy was disappointed to see Father David leave, he'd sat patiently with him on the riverbank in town over a year ago and listened as he told him about the PTSD and his suicide attempt. David had confessed that he couldn't help him. He hadn't understood that listening and caring was all that he'd needed. It was sad that David had left, but understood his reasons for moving on.

This new Priest was a little younger than Andy and had a

young family with four small children. The congregation was hoping it would add new life to the church.

Tina was already murmuring about some changes that he'd made. They'd worked so hard over the last eighteen months, changing mindsets and culture to create a new contemporary service at a more convenient time. It attracted more young families, but Father Grayson began undoing the work the congregation had put in. Andy didn't really care.

What he cared about was what the priest thought when he saw Andy running out of services because of the panic attacks he had in large groups of people.

It was why he'd asked to meet Father Grayson at the riverbank. He checked his watch. It was normal for Andy to get somewhere ten to fifteen minutes early, but sometimes that was a curse. Too much time and the nerves took hold. What right did he have to be here amongst the happy families? He stilled his jiggling leg.

He scanned the area and his eyes rested on Father Grayson.

The youngish man was wearing the black shirt and white collar of his office, smiling and greeting people as he walked past. He'd seemed like a nice enough fella the first time they'd met. Before becoming a priest he'd been a police officer. He gave off that vibe too.

"Andy." Father Grayson extended his hand in greeting.

"Father Grayson. Thanks for coming." Andy returned the handshake.

They sat side by side facing the water. "How can I help you?" Father Grayson angled his body to face Andy.

Andy bent a knee and wrapped his hands around it. Here goes nothing. "I was diagnosed a few months ago with Post Traumatic Stress Disorder. Have you heard of it?"

Father Grayson inclined his head. "Some police officers have it."

"I'm a veteran of Afghanistan and Iraq," Andy continued, telling him about his musicianship as a bagpiper, the soldier deaths and Ramp Ceremonies. The words poured out of his heart, how he'd tried to cope by abusing his body with alcohol, the nightmares he faced every night, his decision to end it all and his belief in God's unexpected rescue. He finished with his treatment through Alice his psychologist.

Father Grayson clasped his hands and held them over his lips as he listened. When the flow of words stemmed he commented, "You need to stop seeing the psychologist. You should come to me or the bishop and repent."

What the —?

Repent for what? Did he do something wrong? Andy shifted back. "Oh. Ah. I'm making a lot of progress with the psychologist. She's been helping me." Maybe the suicide attempt was wrong. Or that he went to war. He stood up and wiped the grass from his backside.

Father Grayson rose with him and dusted off his own rear. "Nevertheless, you would be best to speak with either me or the Bishop."

Andy looked at his watch. "I need to get back home. Tina needed me home to help her with something. And I've taken up enough of your time, Father." It was weird calling a man younger than himself 'Father', but the priest preferred it to 'Grayson'.

They said their farewells and Andy raced back home. He needed Tina. She would help him see where, or if, he had done something wrong.

TINA FINISHED PUTTING THE BOYS' DINNERS ON THEIR PLATES AND put them on the small table in the family room. The front door opened and she heard the sounds of Andy greeting the dogs. Their Great Dane x Ridgeback, Casper, must have stayed on the ground. She was old. The vet suspected that the small lumps that appeared on her body was cancer, but they couldn't afford the tests. He reassured them they would know if she was in any pain.

The Border Collie, Lightning, was a year younger, but being a smaller breed, he had a longer life span. From Andy's frustrated words he was also getting under his feet.

"Casper! Lightning!" She called them as she opened the back door to get their food bowls. "Come and get your dinner!"

"Daddy's home!" Lachie and Callum grabbed a leg each and Andy rubbed their heads and pulled them off.

"Go eat your dinner." He nudged them to the kiddie table.

"Hey, honey," she said through the open door.

"Hey." Andy started unpacking the dishwasher.

She closed the sliding door and left the dogs to their dinner. "How did your meeting with Father Grayson go?"

"Have I done something wrong?" The words seemed to tumble out of his mouth.

"What do you mean?" She grabbed her now cold tea and stuck it in the microwave. Twenty seconds should do it.

"I wanted to meet with Father Grayson to tell him about my PTSD, that if he sees me bolting out of the church, that's why."

"Oh." She knew he'd organised to meet with Father Grayson, but couldn't quite remember why. She pulled her tea out of the microwave and took a sip. "Okay. What did he say?"

His pain-filled brown eyes met hers in confusion. "He said I shouldn't be seeing a psychologist, that I need to speak with either him or the Bishop and repent."

Shock numbed her. "What?!"

"That's what he said."

Why would he say something like that? "Perhaps you misunderstood what he was saying?"

Irritation marred Andy's face. "I know what he said."

She reached out her hand and gently placed it on his arm. "Okay, I believe you. I can't understand why he would say something like that. It just doesn't sound right."

His eyes were stormy with hurt and pain. "Do I need to repent? What have I done wrong?"

"No! You haven't done anything wrong!" She leaned forward.

"You haven't done anything wrong. You didn't ask to get PTSD. This is not your fault."

"But he seems to think it is. Why else would he say I need to repent?"

"Maybe he meant something else?" Tina shrugged a shoulder. "I'm struggling to see why he would say something like that. It doesn't make sense."

Andy's head hung low and a fierce protectiveness filled her heart. "What do I do?"

"I'm not sure."

The conversation played on Tina's mind over and over for the next two weeks. The more she thought about it, the more she didn't like what Father Grayson had said. She made an appointment to speak with him. This last thing was too much. How dare he say Andy shouldn't be getting psychological help. Andy needed to feel safe at church and because of those thoughtless words, this wasn't a place where he was safe.

A few days later, she met with Father Grayson at the church office, setting Callum up in corner of the room with some toys from his backpack.

"I just wanted to let you know that Andy and I will go to another church. There are a few reasons why we want to leave. Changes have been made recently showing us that this church is going in a different direction than we are."

Father Grayson folded his hands on the table and didn't look surprised. Priests often had people saying when they're not happy with the decisions from leadership. But those issues weren't the deal-breaker.

"We're also not happy with what you had to say to Andy when you spoke with him the other week." She tilted her head sideways in curiosity. "What exactly did you mean when you said he shouldn't be seeing a psychologist?"

Father Grayson leaned back in his chair. "Andy doesn't need help from the psychologist. What he needs to do is confess to either myself or the Bishop."

Her jaw slackened. He believed that. Andy was right, he hadn't misunderstood. This person, who was supposed to 'father' them, was not a safe person. Her decision to leave the church cemented further.

They were making the right choice.

"I don't agree with you." Her voice shook when she continued, "And I honestly can't believe that you would suggest such a thing." She held up a hand as he opened his mouth in rebuttal. "But I won't argue with you. That's not why I'm here. I wanted to give you the courtesy of letting you know that we won't be coming back to this church."

Anger and resentment filled her as her need to protect her husband flourished. But she would be polite. She stood up and held out her hand. "Thank you for your time, today. I appreciate it."

Father Grayson stood up with her a clasped her hand looking a little befuddled.

"Callum, I need you to pack up your things, sweetheart." She gathered his bag and frantically shoved toys in. "Callum! Now, please."

Callum and his selective hearing.

She zipped up the bag with shaking hands and took up Callum's free hand. "Come on, darlin', it's time to go to the shops." Her falsely bright tone hid the anger underneath.

"Thanks again, and goodbye," Tina called over her shoulder before the glass door shut behind her. Father Grayson was watching them leave, hands on his hips and mouth slightly open.

ANDY FOUGHT TO KEEP HIS ANXIETY LEVELS UNDER CONTROL AS they parked in the carpark of Overflow Church in Medowie.

Tina hustled the boys out of the car and held their hands while they crossed the bitumen.

The stairs, although only five, each felt like a hurdle.

Tina barreled up them as fast as she could with Callum's three year-old legs beside her. The fast-paced music flowed out the doors as people welcomed them inside.

Andy's heart pounded in time with the heavy drum beat and his breathing escalated. He flung out a hand and caught Tina's arm. "Wait."

She half-turned around, one hand still grasping the glass doors separating the outer room from the larger auditorium.

His shoulders raised up near his ears as he tried to get a deep enough breath. What if he had a panic attack? There were so many people filling the room. His heart thudded.

"Are you okay?"

He hung his head and his shoulders drooped. He had to just suck it up and go in. What kind of man was he that he was afraid to go into a church? He nodded. "I needed a minute. I'll be alright."

"Okay." She smiled a little and opened the door, the music intensifying. She guided the boys through the narrow opening.

He sucked in one last breath and crossed the threshold. A feeling like a warm blanket settled over his shoulders. He exhaled a long breath as peace washed over him. A sense of belonging, of welcome and of safety. He straightened his shoulders and followed Tina to an empty group of chairs directly in front of them.

After the service, the pastor came over and introduced herself. "Hi! It's nice to meet you, I'm Chris. I'm the pastor here." Her friendly and effusive tone set him at ease.

Tina held out her hand and returned the smile. "Hi, I'm Tina. This is my husband Andy, and our two little boys, Lachie and Callum."

Chris greeted the family. "What brought you here today?"

Tina flicked her gaze his way. "Well, we're looking for a new church home. We'd heard good things about this place from friends of ours and we wanted to check it out."

"Okay." Chris nodded and smiled. "Who are your friends, are they here today?"

"Oh no, they don't attend. But you helped them when they were going through a rough time and we remembered how you handled that situation. We respected that, so we wanted to come and see if we'd fit here."

Chris beamed. "That's great." She turned to Andy. "Tell me a little about yourself."

He liked that Chris had included him in the conversation. Quite often at the churches they'd been to over the years, people would talk to Tina because she was friendly and outgoing, but ignore him. As if he were invisible. Someone showing interest in him was rare. "I'm in the RAAF here at Williamtown."

Chris nodded. "We have some RAAF families that attend. I can introduce you, if you want. Have you had a cup of coffee or some morning tea?"

"Not yet." They made their way to the refreshments. Cakes, slices and fresh fruit covered two trestle tables. It was a feast and his stomach reminded him he hadn't eaten breakfast.

Chris connected them with other families to talk to and the feeling of being at home rested in his spirit.

Two weeks later, Andy welcomed Chris into their home.

"I'm sorry I couldn't get here earlier." She'd phoned to say she would be late.

He closed the door behind her. "That's okay. At least this way Lachie and Callum are in bed and we can chat."

At that moment, Tina came from the boy's bedroom. "Hi Chris." She raised an eyebrow and held out her arms, "I'm a hugger, can I have a hug?"

Chris laughed. "I'm hugger too." Andy was surprised when she hugged him as well.

Turning towards the kitchen, Tina asked, "Would you like a cup of tea or coffee?"

"A cup of tea would be lovely, thank you."

"Honey?"

"I'll have a cup of tea, please." He rubbed his suddenly sweaty hands down his pants and motioned to the lounge suite. "Have a seat."

Chris asked how he was finding the church and he commented on how different it was to what he knew.

Tina returned with the tea and sat on the remaining armchair.

Chris took her cup and leaned back in her seat. "What did you want to talk about?"

Tina nodded at Andy to start.

He put the tea down so it didn't betray his trembling hands. "I'm a veteran of Afghanistan and Iraq and I was diagnosed with Post Traumatic Stress Disorder in October last year. I've been seeing a psychologist since—" he cut off his words, almost forgetting Tina knew nothing about his suicide attempt— "then."

Chris sipped her tea as she listened to him describe his treatment and the affect that PTSD had on him. "It sounds like you're making some progress with the psychologist. That's good news."

A burden he didn't know he was carrying lifted from his shoulders. He exchanged a relieved glance with Tina. "That's not what the priest said at our old church when I told him."

Pastor Chris' eye filled with tears as she listened to the advice from their previous spiritual leader. She put down her tea and leaned forward in her chair. "Andy." She placed her hand on her chest. "I want to apologise for what was said to you—"

He interrupted, "You didn't say it."

"I know." Her voice grew thick, "but this person was in a position of spiritual leadership over you. As another spiritual leader, I want to apologise on their behalf."

Tears welled up in his eyes. "I haven't done anything wrong?"

A tear slipped down her cheek. "You haven't done anything wrong, Andy. Getting help for a mental condition isn't wrong."

He wanted to speak, but his mouth refused to form any words.

Tina came back into the room with a tissue box, he didn't

know she'd left. "I thought we might need these." She offered the tissue box around and they all laughed through their tears.

They spoke for another hour, and each minute reaffirmed that this faith community, with this leader, was where they belonged.

9

—————

Andy collected his mug from the small coffee table and took it through the kitchen. He'd been in the shower earlier and his heart burned to tell Tina about the idea that had been plaguing him.

Back in the lounge room, he sat down in front of the TV and drummed his hands on his thigh. Finally, she came back through after putting the boys to bed.

He stilled his hands. "Are they asleep?"

She collapsed on the single seater. "Yep. It took forever."

He'd felt every minute. Now was the time to bring his idea up. He fiddled with the TV remote.

"What are you watching?"

He had no idea. "Uh, nothin', I was just flicking through the channels."

"I'm sorry we didn't get to talk much earlier."

He liked to debrief with Tina about his day when he came home from work, but with a six-year old and a three-year old constantly interrupting, it drove him nuts. His fist clenched. He hated coming last in her attention. He shrugged. "Yeah."

"Did you want to finish talking about it now?"

"Nah, there wasn't much else to say." His heart burned again.

"Actually, can I ask you something?" He didn't wait for a response. "I feel like there's something I'd like to do and I want to know if you think I should do it or not. I kinda think that maybe it's something my new faith is behind." The words tumbled out over themselves in embarrassment. What if he had it all wrong?

Tina's eyebrows quirked and she gave a half-grin. "Sure."

"I want to raise awareness for PTSD, especially for veterans. I want to break the stigma in society around mental health. Men don't talk about this stuff. We think that to say you need help is a sign of weakness. I suffered for four years before I got help because of it." His voice strengthened with each passionate word. "The plan is to walk on Manly Beach in the soft sand. Walk one kilometre and carry one kilogram for every Australian solider that died over there." He held his breath.

Tina focused inwardly for a moment. "Yeah, okay. This is what you need to do. How many kilometres will you have to walk?"

"We've lost 39 soldiers, so I'd walk 39 kilometres and carry 39 kilograms in my field pack."

"Why Manly Beach, and not one of the ones here?"

He'd considered that, but rejected it. "I'm familiar with it. Remember, I used to be a lifeguard on the beach when I was in my early twenties. I know exactly how long it is, and how many laps I need to do. Manly Beach always has people around, even in the middle of winter."

"Do you have a date in mind?"

"Yeah, June seventh."

"Have you thought about how you'll train for it?"

He'd already worked it all out. "I'll go to the Stockton Sand Dunes, and train out there. I'll go with just my webbing to start with." The harness with pockets would be useful for carrying food. "I'll need to replace my Camelbak, invest in some good quality boots so I don't tear my feet up training."

Tina's eyes looked to be glazing over as he flooded her with details. "When are you going to fit this training in? Is it going to be taking away from our family time? You know how I feel about that." She was very protective of their time together.

"No, I'll be able to train 2-3 times during the week doing shorter distances. I'm allowed time every day for physical training. Then, I'll do a longer walk on Saturdays. But I'll get up early before it gets too hot and be home early. I'll start out small and then build my way up to the longer distances, and slowly increase the weights I carry too." His background as a triathlete helped him understand how to train for long events, to break it all down and build his way up. It was how he'd gone from the smaller triathlons to the longer Ironman events.

Tina's expression turned thoughtful. "Okay. Let's do this, then. The boys and I will support you all the way." The love in her eyes warmed his heart.

He smiled back, tentatively. He could do this, right?

A couple of nights later, they were discussing the walk again. "I need a name for it. You're a writer, can you come up with anything?"

"Nothing that doesn't sound stupid. 'Manly Beach Walk for PTSD'?"

"Yeah, nah." He shook his head, a smile playing around his mouth.

She laughed.

"I was telling Foxy about it this morning. He came up with '39 for 39'. 39 kms and kilos for 39 Aussie soldiers who have died in the war."

Tina half-smiled. "I like the name, it rolls off the tongue." She frowned and stared through him. "Actually," her sad blue eyes met his. "I think it's going to be '40 for 40'.

"What?" He sat up straighter. "Did we lose another one?"

"I haven't heard anything. I have a feeling it will be '40 for 40'."

A few days later another solider died.

ANDY PULLED THE CAR INTO THE CARPARK AND GRABBED HIS webbing from the back. He pocketed the keys and put on the Camelbak drink container. Its backpack style with long attached mouthpiece slung over his shoulder and he pulled it tight.

He could just make out the path in front of him in the dark as he made his way along the well-worn track to the dunes. The hint of dawn lightened the horizon as he took his first steps on the soft sand.

It was his first Saturday training session. He'd gone out on Tuesday for the first time with his workmate Jed.

The sky lightened further as Andy's calves burned, but the peace that filled him made the discomfort bearable. He dug the toes of his boots into the dune. At the top the view stole his breath. A certainty filled the air. This was the right thing to do. How many soldiers and veterans would never get to see another sunrise? Tears stung his eyes, blurring the beautiful sight, and he blinked them away. Comfort settled over him and he broke down in the safe space.

The sun was a little higher in the sky when he wiped the evidence of his emotional breakdown off his face and shoved the water mouthpiece into his mouth. Drawing deeply, he drank the icy cold water and stepped off the top of the dune and jogged down other side.

Months passed by and the training sessions blended into each other. Each time going further and longer, the weight that he carried heavier and heavier.

"YOU WON'T BELIEVE WHAT HAPPENED TODAY AT THE DUNES." ANDY announced to Tina on a Tuesday when he got home from work. He fumbled in his pocket for his keys and dropped them into the bowl, his stomach a ball of anticipation and nerves.

"What happened?" She dried her hands on a tea towel.

He followed her to the kitchen. Where did he start? "I got a

call from The Examiner asking if they could do an article on me."
How had the local paper even heard about his 40 for 40 walk?

"No way."

He smiled, still amazed. "They wanted to meet me at the dunes when I went for my training session today."

Tina hung up the towel and turned back to him, leaning against the kitchen bench. "How did they even find out what you're doing?"

He shook his head in disbelief. "I'm not sure. They asked me a bunch of questions about when it will be and why I was doing it."

"That's awesome."

Callum ran into the kitchen and back out again, pretending to fight enemies that only existed in his imagination.

There was still so much to do. He envisioned how he wanted the beach set up for the walk and he didn't know how it would happen. "I want to put photos up of the Australian soldiers who died in the Middle East along the beach. I want them set up in a row."

"How big do you want the photos to be?"

He'd looked up sizes the other day and saw it would be expensive. He told her the size he wanted and how much.

"We don't have that kind of money laying around."

He was hoping she'd say no worries, but as a one income family they could only dream of luxuries. "I also want to get some of those little Australian flags to put on the beach. One to represent every solider who's taken their life since 2000." He took a breath and exhaled. "There's been 97 suicides of veterans."

"I'm not sure if you'll be able to get them, shops usually only have stuff like that around Australia Day. Ask if they any stock left over."

He shrugged. "I can try."

A few days later, he approached the customer service desk at the local BIG W. "Can I please speak to a manager?"

The woman took a slight step back and asked, "Is it something I can help you with?"

"I need ninety-seven of those little Australian flags, the ones you guys sell around Australia Day. Is that something that you can help me with?"

She raised an eyebrow curiously and smiled. "I'll page the manager for you."

"Thanks."

Before long, a man came towards him and Andy explained what he needed. "I'm doing a walk to raise awareness for Post Traumatic Stress Disorder. I'll be walking 40 kilometres carrying 40 kilograms, one for every soldier we lost in the Middle East. The flags up on the beach I'd like to set up in formation to represent one flag for every soldier suicide since 2000. Is it possible to get some of those little Aussie flags, or do you have any left over from Australia Day?"

Compassionate, wide eyes met his. "Wow. How many do you need?"

"Ninety-seven."

His hazel eyes filled with sorrow. "That's a lot of suicides. I'll order them in for you."

The tension in Andy's shoulders eased. "Thank you. How much will it cost?"

The manager waved his hands. "No charge. We love to do things for charities. Is there anything else that you were looking to get from us? We'd love to help you out any way that we can."

Was he serious? "Ah, yeah. I wanted to get large photos of each of the soldiers who died so that the public can see the faces of those we lost to war. But that will be expensive."

"Don't worry about the cost." The manager waved his hand. "I'll look after it. How many photos do you need?"

"There are 40 soldiers. How should I order it, do I just go to the counter?"

"Put the photos on a USB drive and ask to see me."

His throat tight with suppressed emotion, Andy stuck out his hand. "Thank you so much, for this." He fought back the tears that threatened. The generosity was overwhelming.

The manager grasped his hand and walked him out of the shop. "No, thank you. Thank you for what you're doing." He paused and waved a finger as if he'd had an idea. "I bet Colleen and Stewart will want to know about this."

Andy looked at him blankly. Who?

"Colleen and Stewart are the managers for the Raymond Terrace Marketplace shopping centre. They love getting involved in charities and helping out people like yourself. I'll have a chat with them about it."

"That would be awesome. Thank you."

He wasn't sure what they could do to help, but he wouldn't deny any type of support.

November 2013

ANDY STARED, AMAZED. THURSDAY NIGHT AND THE SHOPPING centre was packed. A large group congregated in the food court for the raffle and the silent auction.

Large posters of himself, promoting his '40 for 40' walk were displayed around the Marketplace. Colleen, Stewart and Joe had gone above and beyond in their support. They were holding a silent auction with the funds raised going towards his nominated non-profit that supported veterans with PTSD. The items donated from the various shops spread across a fold-up table on one side of the raffle barrel.

He wiped his clammy hands. Soon he would speak about his experience with PTSD.

Tina was by the travelator watching Callum as he journeyed up and down the ramps. It was difficult keeping the active four year old entertained. He was too much like his mother, easily distracted. Seven year-old Lachie was next to her, content to watch the people.

The raffle wound up and Colleen handed him the

microphone. His hand trembled and he clenched his fist tighter so it didn't fall.

He inhaled a deep breath. Peace descended over him. He raised the microphone to his chin. "Good evening. My name is Andrew Summers. I'm a Corporal in the Royal Australian Air Force. Colleen and Stewart invited me to speak about my experiences tonight. You may have seen the posters." He waved his free hand all around. Soft laughter flowed through the crowd. The posters *were* difficult to miss. "I completed two tours of Afghanistan and Iraq and I came home with Post Traumatic Stress Disorder." He continued, telling the listeners about the Ramp Ceremonies, his nightmares and flashbacks. The audience hung on every word. Several shoppers walking past stopped.

He took a quick swallow of water as he fought the words he felt burning within.

Tell them. The 'voice' he associated with God prodded him. *Tell them about the suicide attempt.*

Really? Now? He hadn't even told Tina. He slumped his shoulders, replacing the water bottle. He'd promised to do what God asked of him.

Clearing his throat, he continued, "I got to the lowest point at my brother-in-law's wedding. My wife was still at the reception, and the boys were in bed when I tried to commit suicide." A hush enveloped the space and he fought to maintain eye-contact with the crowd. "I had a bottle of whisky and all the pills in the cupboard. I was going to end it all. My family deserved to have a better husband and father." He wanted to find Tina in the crowd, but he couldn't bear to meet her gaze. "As I was saying my goodbyes to the pictures of my family on the TV cabinet, I heard my wife's voice in my head telling me about her faith in God. I stopped and got down on my knees." His voice trembled. "And I said to God that if He was real like my wife said, then I asked Him to save me. I gave Him twenty-four hours to do it."

Need overtook the shame and he met his wife's stunned eyes.

He what? Why was she only hearing about this now? Tina struggled to comprehend her husband's confession.

Andy's eyes met hers and the pleading and shame in his brown depths pulled her out of herself. She gave him an encouraging nod and a sad smile.

He took another breath and finished. "I set aside the tablets and the whisky and thought, I can always come back again tomorrow night. My wife went to church the next day and she met an Army psychologist who just happened to be passing through."

Tears flooded her eyes and a swirl of emotion engulfed her. She swallowed them back. Now wasn't the time.

Andy thumped his chest. "Now I took that as my prayer was answered, and I want to encourage anyone here tonight. If you feel as if you can't do it anymore. If you feel like the only way out is to end it, I want to tell you there's another way. The next day I went to work. That Army psychologist put me in touch with the psychologist I see now. If you are suffering at all from any kind of mental health problem, I strongly encourage you to get help. There are so many places that you can get help. Google Lifeline. Or Beyond Blue. But get help. It doesn't have to be the end."

Pride swelled her chest and she mentally prayed for anyone in the shopping centre who was contemplating suicide, asking God to intervene for them, like she believed He'd intervened for her husband and thanked Him for saving Andy.

Andy had finished and made his way over to her. He pulled her in for a tight hug. "I'm so sorry that I didn't tell you. I was ashamed." The words muffled into her shoulder.

"It's okay." She drew back and met his distraught eyes. "I understand." She did. She hadn't told him about the time she'd contemplated sticking her head in the oven. But this wasn't the time to tell him. They'd both been bad at communicating the important issues. That needed to change. How hard it would have been to admit to his wife, someone he wanted to think the best of him, that he had nearly left her a widow and her children fatherless. By choice. She rubbed his arm. "We can talk about it more later."

He nodded and turned back to the people who wanted to speak with him.

She let Lachie and Callum play around the open area. It was nearly closing time and the majority of shops would soon be closed. There was only a handful of people left when she noticed Lachie and Callum begin to lose energy.

She caught Andy's attention and waved her head towards the boys. He jerked his head up in understanding. She called out to Lachie and Callum, "Five more minutes, boys, and then we can go home."

Lachie wandered back towards her and Callum trailed along behind. His favourite place to be, right next to his older brother. Holding onto Callum's hand, Tina brought the family back together.

"Thank you so much for doing this." Andy gave Colleen, Stewart and Joe a hug. The three of them had worked hard to bring the night about.

"It's our pleasure, Andy." Colleen smiled and opened her arms for Tina. "We'll count the money raised in the morning and get a total for you. Do you want us to give the money to you, or put it directly on the GoFundMe page?"

The GoFundMe page had become a necessary early on as people were moved both by Andy's story and the many other Veterans that suffered with PTSD. People wanted to contribute in some way. Andy started up the page so people could contribute financially if they chose to a non-profit that helped Veterans.

"If you wouldn't mind doing that for me, then it will show up on the GoFundMe page that the donation is from you all, otherwise it will look like I've donated it."

When the boys were settled into bed sometime later, Tina thought back on the shock of Andy's words. Attempted suicide.

It both broke her heart and yet he was with them, so she was glad. She didn't know what to make of the maelstrom within, because it had all happened more than a year earlier. Andy was getting better. She knew he wasn't in that place anymore. But he had been.

Thank You so much, Lord. I didn't know, but You did and You saved him. Thank you.

She remembered coming home from church with the exciting news, and Andy's strange reaction, 'God's real,' he'd said. At the time, she remembered being confused by his words, but now it all made sense.

Andy's words from earlier that evening came to mind, 'My family deserved to have a better husband and father.'

Another memory swamped her. She'd been so excited by her weight-loss that she wanted to show off her new body to Andy. His response had been strange. 'You could have any guy you want,' he'd said. It dawned on her he'd meant when he was gone.

A sob caught her off-guard. She'd nearly lost him, and she'd had no idea.

He'd planned to take his life and she had been oblivious. She racked her brains, there must have been other signs. But nothing came to mind.

Inhaling a deep breath, she came back through to the lounge room where Andy watched TV. His usual position these days. Gone were the days of him cleaning up and contributing to the everyday chores. It was so hard to remember, but she dared not dwell on it too long. He was a different person, nothing like the man she'd married.

PTSD had changed him in so many ways. When was the last time he'd teased her? Laughed? Played with their boys? Her sadness deepened. Been intimate? She wasn't so skinny anymore. All her focus was on getting through the days, bearing the load of the family's needs so exercise was non-existent. But she had needs too. Intimacy was another way of saying 'I love you'. Was she unattractive to him? Or was the PTSD taking away his desire? She studied him as he zoned into the TV show. It was tempting to be angry. To rage at the unfairness of it all. The disorder had robbed them all of so much. And it had almost taken from her the one she was supposed to grow old with.

But it wasn't Andy's fault he had PTSD. She knew the darkness of a mental health issue and thought of her own contemplation of suicide a few years earlier. Her shoulders fell, remembering that dark place. She didn't know he'd been there. Too.

10

Manly, Sydney
7ᵗʰ June, 2014

The quiet vibration of the phone's alarm woke Tina up at 3:45am. She rubbed her face and stretched. Nerves tingled and danced along her skin at the not-knowing what the day would bring.

So many elements came together for the '40 for 40'. People from Andy's work volunteering their weekend to support him and collect money for the non-profit. Friends from church giving up their time to support Andy and to speak with those who want to talk about mental health issues, praying for those that want prayer.

Close friends and family were coming as well to support her, so she could support Andy. Since they were helping watch the boys, she would devote all her time and attention to what he needed.

Andy didn't know she felt guilty. She wanted to give more of herself when he was struggling. Wanted to be the one to go with him to his psychologist appointments, but with young children to care for, it wasn't possible. This one day she would be the support that he needed.

Andy came out of the shower and she rolled out of bed.

They packed their things together, careful not to wake the boys. Andy's father was coming to watch over them while they slept. After waking, they would all meet at the beach.

Andy looked at his watch again. "Dad's not here yet. Maybe you should stay here."

Nope. Not happening. "Let's just wait and see, what time is it?"

"4:15."

"He's still got time. You told him to get here for 4:30."

"Okay." Andy blew out a breath. "I'll double check I've got everything."

A soft knock on the door relaxed her shoulders. Andy raced to the door. "Hey, Dad."

"Hello, son." Owen's soft Scottish brogue came through the doorway. He gave Andy a hug and came into the room. "Hello, Tina." His thin frame enveloped her in a firm hug.

"Good morning." She stepped back and said softly, "The boys were up late last night, so I'm not sure what time they'll wake. They usually get out of bed early, around 6:30-7am, but they may sleep in. Breakfast—"

"Dad'll work it out, we need to get going," Andy interrupted.

He's just anxious. She let it go. "Okay." He wasn't the only nervous one.

Out on the street in front of the boardwalk, they met the RAAF contingent of the support team.

"Thank you so much guys," Andy said, as his work mates carried equipment from the vehicle.

"No worries, Summo. Where do you want us to set up this stuff?"

Andy pointed down the stairs to the sand right in front of them. "If you set up the marquee there and line the photographs along the beach around this area." He motioned with his hands. "I want the Aussie flags lined up in rows and columns like on a parade ground."

"No worries. We'll get on it. Where do you want the buckets for donations?"

"If you have some on the table under the marquee, that will be fine."

Alice stood waiting in the distance. Andy beamed when he saw her. "Hey, Alice. You didn't have to come."

"I said that I would, so here I am."

She couldn't believe Alice was there so early in the morning.

Alice met her gaze and silently communicated with her eyes. She nodded back because she wasn't quite sure what she was asking. Was he okay? Nervous, pre-race jitters? Yes. Was this going to be difficult for him? Yes, and not just physically.

At five o'clock, Andy stepped off the start line. Next to him were some work colleagues who had opted to walk several laps with him. The rest lined up at the start, clapping and cheering. Andy ducked his head and waved his hand high to acknowledge them.

By the time the sun was up, the marquee was in the place, the photos of soldiers who paid the ultimate price in war lined up facing the crowds. Next to them, the flags. Her heart gripped tight at the sight of so many flags representing the suicides.

Andy was almost one of those flags.

Back and forth he trudged along the beach. Each time passing the photos the weight of his 40kg field pack seemed to weigh heavier and heavier.

The boys soon came down the beach. "Mummy! Mummy!" They tore across the sand to her and each clung onto a different side.

"Hey, sweethearts. Have you been having a good time with Grandpa?"

"Yep!"

"What time did you wake up?"

Lachie shrugged. "I don't know."

"Have you been awake for a long time, or just a little bit?"

"About medium."

She laughed. "Okay."

Callum, distracted by the flags reached out and plucked one from the sand. She lunged for him and pointed to the rest of them. "Callum, you need to put that back, darlin'. They're not for playing with. It's a very serious thing."

"Why?" The question of all pre-schoolers everywhere.

"Because it's something to do with Daddy's walk. Just leave it alone, please."

She spent more time with them while waiting for Andy to return from his last lap. He started out strong, but the emotional weight looked to be taking more out of him. How many laps had he done? Was he due for a rest break?

Family and friends arrived and took over watching Lachie and Callum.

Members of their church arrived, holding buckets for donations and speaking with passers-by about the event. Pastor Chris, John, Brian, Helen and the others chatted with strangers about mental health, and prayed with those who wished for prayer.

She made her way back to the starting point where the support marquees were set up with a masseuse table and a tarp hanging down for privacy.

"How's he going?" One of the support team asked.

"I'm hoping Andy's going to have rest after this last lap, he looks like he's tiring."

Andy came back down the beach, different people walking with him now, including Danie and Vicky from church.

"Are you having a rest now?" she asked him. The camouflaged bandana wrapped around his bald head dripped with sweat, rivulets running down the sides of his face.

"Yeah." He dropped the pack and it thudded on the sand.

With a heavy step he went for a massage. He lay on his stomach while a work colleague trained as a masseuse began working on his calves.

"Have you had anything to eat, yet?" she asked, concerned that she hadn't seen him eat.

"Just a couple of lollies."

She made a face at him. "That's not enough. You can't expect your body to do this if you're don't give it the fuel it needs."

Andy gave a weary half-laugh, half-groan. "You sound like Anthony used to. When I did the triathlons, I didn't eat much either. My friends were always telling me to eat more. But I just can't. The thought of food just makes me feel sick."

"You need to eat something. You can't do this without food. Is there anything that you think you could stomach?"

"Lollies." He groaned as the masseuse focussed on a section of his calf muscle.

"Very funny. Real food."

"I don't know. A banana?"

She searched in the supply bag of food for a banana and pulled it out. "What distance have you done so far?"

"That last lap took me up to 20kms." By lunch time? It impressed her he was just now beginning to tire.

"I'll walk this next lap with you."

So far he hadn't had to do a single lap alone. There was always someone there next to him trudging along in the sand.

The masseuse left the small makeshift room to allow him to cover up in privacy.

She thrust the banana at Andy as he got up from the table. "Here. Eat this."

He took it from her, peeled the skin back, broke off half and gave the rest back to her.

"What are you doing?"

"I need to get back out there." He shoved on the webbing and leaned down to hoist the 40kg field pack on his back.

"You haven't had much of a rest."

His eyes were serious. "I have to finish this. I'm starting to get tired, which means that it's going to take longer for me to get to the end. I probably won't finish until after it gets dark."

"Don't forget your plan B."

TINA DIDN'T UNDERSTAND. HE NEEDED TO DO THIS. IT WAS A GOOD idea having a plan B, but Andy was going to do everything in his power to make sure he didn't need it.

He adjusted the heavy pack onto his shoulders and it settled more comfortably on his back. His muscles strained with the familiar weight. The banana was thick and gross in his mouth, but he ate it to appease his wife.

The idea of eating swirled up the nausea in his gut. He washed the banana taste out of his mouth with the cool water Tina refilled.

They set out again on the soft sand. The area had filled up with many people, but it was a blur of noise and colour. His body ached. His feet were getting tender, he'd noticed some red patches of blisters beginning to form.

He readjusted the pack while his gaze fixed on the staked photos. One foot in front of the other. This was why he was doing it. For them.

He slowed down and stared into the eyes of each soldier. Killed in Action. Their death was not in vain and he wouldn't allow the public to continue to think that it was.

He increased his pace as he past the flags, raising his hand to the bluetooth earphones, ready to zone out to his playlist.

"How you goin', Summo?"

Andy paused his hand, dropping it as he turned to his work mate.

"Yeah. Not too bad." If he didn't focus on the pain. Tight muscles protested and complained. He answered the questions that continued to flow, but he had trouble taking in the words.

The workmate dropped behind to walk with others, joining them for the lap. Tina kept in step beside him and another person moved closer. He lifted his hand to press the earphone button.

And dropped it again. "What distance are you up to now, Summo?"

He must have answered cause the guy nodded in response. He said something else and he must have responded appropriately but he didn't know what the conversation was about. They fell into silence. Once again, he lifted his hand to start the playlist when the guy launched into another topic. Was he trying to distract him? Tina gave him a sympathetic look. She was on the side that had the 'on' button on his earphones and saw him trying to get into the zone.

When the guy fell back to join the others, it was just the two of them. He reached for his music as Tina leaned in close. "It's okay to tell them that you don't want to talk."

"I know, I feel bad 'cause they want to encourage me."

Her eyebrows raised. "They aren't the ones walking 40kms carrying 40kgs. You don't have to be rude, just say that you need to get into your zone and turn on your music. It will help take your mind off the pain."

He nodded.

"I'm going to shut up now so you can put your music on," she said, with a self-deprecating laugh.

Finally, music blasted in his ears and he trudged to the beat. He didn't take his eyes off the pale sand in front of him. He'd worn a decent track into the sand and he tried to step in the footprints he'd already made. He rolled his shoulders to ease the ache. The weight seemed heavier than the last lap. Each step caused a deep ache in his body.

One more lap. Then the next.

The steps blurred together as the warmth of the day passed and evening approached. He couldn't keep the pain from twisting his features as headed for the little base camp. His quads and hamstrings seized. Sharp, knife-like pain seared him. Ahead the photos of soldiers no longer on the earth called him forward. One foot. Another.

He collapsed in front of the row of soldiers, like a turtle laying on its back. Fire erupted in his leg. Squeezing his eyes shut, he tried to breathe out the pain.

Hands rubbed at his legs through the camouflaged material. Tears leaked from his eyes and he tried to cover his face. The pain gradually eased but doubts about his ability to finish continued to taunt him.

He hobbled over to the marquee and fell on the cot.

"Hey Summo, is there anything I can do for you?" A voice penetrated the exhaustion.

He groaned and threw his arm over his face. "Yeah, can you grab my wife for me?"

"Sure, mate." Footsteps faded away.

Tina threw aside the side flap. "Oh my gosh, it's so hot in here. Do you want me to open up the sides?"

"Nah. I want some privacy."

"Okay. You want some food?"

His stomach roiled in protest both hungry and sick. "No, I can't eat." She didn't look impressed. He tried to distract her. "Did you see the news people earlier?"

"Yeah, I was here when they turned up."

"Did you see what channel it was?"

"We've had a couple actually. Channel 7 couldn't hang around for you to get back from your lap, but they'll try to come back later. Channel 10 was the one who interviewed you."

"It'll be on the news tonight. I'll still be walking."

"You think it will take that long?"

"Yeah." He flung an arm out. "It's taken all this time to get to 30kms."

"Wow. Only ten to go."

He snorted, *only ten*, she said. He bent down and removed his boots. "Yeah, but it's ten kilometres with these." He thrust his red, swollen and torn-up feet at her.

"Oh, crap."

Wasn't the word he would've chosen, but yeah. Crap. "I don't think I can do anymore with my feet like this."

Tina stared at him as if to try to guess his thoughts. "Do you want to go ahead with Plan B?"

"I don't know." It tore at his guts to depend on others. This was his mission. Plan B felt like failure. They'd decided earlier when planning the event what to do if he became injured and couldn't finish. It involved volunteers carrying the 40kg pack on a stretcher for the remainder of the 40kms. They'd also planned on carrying him on a stretcher, but there was no way that would happen.

"This was why we had a Plan B in place, if for any reason you couldn't complete the 40kms by yourself." She shrugged. "It's up to you."

"Would the boys want to do it?" His workmates had already volunteered earlier, but now that it was time… would they still?

"I can find out. Do you want me to send Alice in here?"

"Yeah, that'd be good." Alice would help. He knew beforehand the walk would drain emotionally. Just not how much.

Alice came in and asked him a few questions. She admonished him for staring at the photos every time he walked past because of the emotional pain. How could he tell her that he couldn't look away? They were the very reason he was walking in the first place. She left when Tina came back in and they had a few quiet words on the edge of the tent.

Tina entered fully as Alice left. "The guys have actually been rehearsing for a stretcher carry on your last lap. They got bored so they practised changing over positions." She settled down next to him. "So, if you do go ahead, what will it look like? Are you going on the stretcher?"

He shook his head adamantly. "No. Not me, the field pack. I'll keep walking."

"Ah. I like that."

"Like what?"

"I like that it's a way of saying it's okay to need help. To reach out to others when you need to. It takes a lot of courage to accept help. You can show people what that looks like."

He couldn't meet her eyes. "Feels like a cop out."

"It's not a cop out, and it takes far more character to say you need help than breaking yourself in the process. Isn't your whole message about getting help for mental health?"

"Yeah." It still tasted like failure.

Silence filled the tent for a few minutes. "I'll support you no matter what you choose."

"I don't want to put people out."

"You won't put them out." She pointed in the general direction of his workmates. "They *want* to help you."

"If I continued alone, we'd be here all night." At his current pace, that wasn't an exaggeration.

She caught his eye, though he tried to evade it. "Then we'll be here all night. We're here for you as long as this takes. Even if no one else stays, I'm here for you."

He nodded. Buoyed by the support, yet weighed down with failure. He broke eye contact and studied the sand.

Her next words were soft. "You have to think about why you're here; what's your purpose in doing this walk. 'Cause if you're doing this as an achievement, then keep going. But if it's raising awareness for PTSD, to encourage other people who are struggling to get help, then I can't think of a better way to tell people, than to be an example." She straightened. "Pastor Chris talked about this possibility with you two weeks ago, do you want me to get her?"

Her words sat heavy on his soul. "Yeah, that would be good."

She stopped in front of him and reached out for his hand. He drew his eyes unwillingly to hers. "I love you and I'm so proud of you. This must be hard for you, but I know that you can do it. You are courageous, and you don't shy away from doing the hard things." She gave a final squeeze and left him to his thoughts.

Pastor Chris came through the tent not long after and sat next to him on the massage table. "Hey, Andy. How are you going?"

"Not good."

"Tell me what's going on."

"I've just hit 30kms, and I'm struggling to continue. My feet are torn up and I'm cramping too bad to carry the 40kgs."

Chris nodded, responding in her wise and compassionate way. "Isn't this why you have men here to help? Men who are so keen on helping you, they've spent the last half an hour practising using the stretcher." Her eyes seemed to pierce his soul. "It's not failure to accept help. You are not a burden on anyone. We are all here to support you in whatever way you need support. What a way to show people how to accept help and support from others!"

"It's hard, Chris. I said that I would do it and I feel like I'm letting everyone down."

"We might have plans and ideas on how things work out, but didn't we discuss that sometimes God shapes the outcome differently to what we want or expect?"

"What do you mean?"

"Well, what if God wants you to *show* people what reaching out for help looks like, even when it's hard, when it feels like you've failed? Leaders lead the way."

Her words resonated within. A mix of emotions, relief, unworthiness and despair tangled in his gut. He should've been able to do this without assistance, but if it meant helping more people, he would do it. "Okay," He rose up on weary, shaky legs. "Let's finish this."

———

TINA'S GAZE TRACKED CHRIS AS SHE MADE HER WAY TOWARDS HER awkwardly in the soft sand. "He's going to get the guys on the stretcher to help."

Relief blew out the breath she'd held. Her shoulders slumped, and head tilted up to the clouds. "Thank God." She met Chris' brown eyes. "Thank you. I think he needed to hear that it was okay from someone he sees as being in authority. He needed to hear it from you."

Chris pulled her close and squeezed her tight. So much love and compassion in one quick hug.

Andy hobbled out of the tent with his head down. He'd sacrificed his pride, and he looked ashamed.

Oh no. Not on her watch.

She marched over and stood directly before him, shoes touching.

He glanced up.

"You're going to accept the help?"

"Yeah." He studied his boots again.

She lifted his chin with her fingers. "I'm so proud of you."

His eyes flashed with an emotion she couldn't describe and he ducked his head again.

She tilted his chin again, but he kept his eyes downward. "Honey?" She tried again.

Her breath caught at the despair and defeat flooding his milk-chocolate eyes. "What?" He shifted his feet awkwardly.

She let go of his chin, but not the problem. "You are not a failure."

His head ducked again. "Yeah, I know."

"No, you don't."

His gaze slammed up to hers.

"You don't believe that. You think you've failed."

"I can't finish this without help."

"But what you're doing is setting an example on how to reach out for the help that's there. It's far more important than saying you've finished by yourself."

He toed the sand. "Yeah."

She wanted this to sink in. "Repeat after me, 'I am not a failure.'"

He rolled his eyes at her.

She cocked an eyebrow. "Say it."

"I am not a failure," he mumbled.

"You don't mean that. Try again."

"I am not a failure." He stared at her with a 'really?' expression.

"Louder."

"I am not a failure."

"Say it like you mean it." She poked him in the chest.

"I AM NOT A FAILURE."

She smiled. "Better." Pulling him close for a hug, she repeated, "I am so proud of you. I can see it was difficult for you to make this choice. It's taken a lot of courage, and you're showing me and the world, that this walk isn't about you. It's about your message."

ANDY SHOOK HIS HEAD AND DREW TINA CLOSER FOR ANOTHER tight hug. She was nuts at times, but her heart was beautiful. "Thank you."

"Oh!" Tina grabbed his arm as he was about to turn away. "Alice said to tell you to stop looking at the photographs on your way past. She's noticed that it's getting to you more and more."

His lips quirked. "Yeah, she told me, too." But he would still pay his respects. It was a major reason he was there, to honour them and their sacrifice. "I need to honour them, what they sacrificed."

"Aren't you already doing that by walking? Not looking at their pictures won't change anything, except put your head in a better headspace."

He nodded, but deep down he knew there was no way he

could walk past the images without giving them the honour they deserved.

After some quick practises with the weight of the pack on the stretcher, Andy called everyone, work colleagues, church friends, and family together. "I want to say thank you. This is hard for me to do, because to me, that pack represents each one of those soldiers." He pointed towards the photographs behind him. "But I want to thank you for stepping up and helping me to finish my mission and show people that they can reach out and accept assistance from others. Let's get these last ten clicks done."

"Yea!" A few people clapped in encouragement. The stretcher carry team made sure the pack was secure and on the count of three lifted up the heavy load.

"Let's go."

Tina walked in step with him and grabbed his hand. She squeezed it once and he reflexively squeezed back before she dropped it. Her support meant the world to him. The sunlight was fading quickly and he hobbled along.

The stretcher team called out for a transition to the next team, and it smoothly changed hands. The old team shook their arms and loosened tight muscles while they continued. "Summo, I don't know how you managed to carry that for 30 clicks, man," one of them called out.

He shrugged. "I've been training for this for over twelve months. You guys haven't, so it should be easier for me. I didn't start with the field pack, and it didn't weigh 40kgs either."

Not carrying it now felt strange. The lightness was more than physical, it was a lightness in his spirit that wasn't there before.

The sun sank further towards the horizon and by the second-last lap, the muscles that had been happier without the pack were screaming at him again. His feet burned with every aching step. The sting became sharper and sharper until he had to stop and sit in the cooling sand. "I've got to stop for a sec." He mumbled the words.

"Okay." Tina turned to the group as he collapsed, sitting on the sand off to the side. "Guys, take a few minutes."

"I've got to check my feet," he said to her.

One of the guys asked, "Is everything alright?"

Tina walked over to where they'd set the stretcher down. "Andy needs to check his feet."

He reached over to undo his laces, but his leg cramped. "Aaarrgh!"

Tina rushed back over, but another mate had already bent down and begun to take his boot off. The boots had torn across the top, looking like they were years old instead of only a few months. A sharp sting stabbed at his feet. He held his breath.

He lay back on the sand, resting his back on a large mound. It felt like his skin was being peeled off with the sock. He was glad he couldn't contort himself to look, he didn't want to see it, anyway.

"Ah, Summo. Mate. Why didn't you tell us earlier?"

"How bad is it?"

His colleague waved the blood-soaked sock in front of him. He jerked his head back. "Oh, that stinks."

His mate laughed. "Yep, it's pretty gross. I think I need a gas mask," he joked.

Tina leaned closer but abruptly backed away. "That's disgusting."

The look or the stink? "Is the smell as bad as when I'd been away for weeks out bush with the infantry?"

"It's worse." Her voice was nasal, fingers pinching her nostrils.

"I didn't think that was possible."

"Me neither."

"Ready, Summo?" A water bottle was poised over the open wounds on his tender feet.

He nodded. "Go." His breath hissed out.

"You want the boot back on, mate?"

"Nah, I'll let the air dry it first."

The laces on the other boot loosened and he grimaced,

engulfed in waves of pain. More needle-like stabs as the sock ripped away layers of skin.

"Ah, mate. Your toe nails are turning black."

He didn't want to know that. He had to continue. Maybe taking the boots off hadn't been a good idea.

Tina held up a boot and sand poured out in a steady stream. "I think I've found out why your toes are getting bruised, there's no room left in your boot for your feet. How the heck did the sand even get in your boot in the first place?"

Andy pointed to the holes across the top of the toe area. He hissed again as the water cleaned off the other foot. They didn't bring anything to clean his feet with, so water would have to suffice.

"Ah. That'd do it." For an intelligent woman, it surprised him the basic stuff he had to point out to her.

"What are you going to do?"

He raised his brows. "Put my boots back on."

Conflict warred on her face, but she nodded.

Getting the boots back on was worse, but they needed to keep moving on. One more lap after this. The sun was barely visible on the horizon and the night air was cooling them down too much.

He held out his hand and they pulled him back to his feet.

They headed out to the furthest point and turned back to the start.

By the time the last of the thirteen laps begun, a small crew had joined him. Work mates and church friends alike.

His Dad. Having his parent's support meant everything. Mum couldn't walk on the sand because of her health, but Tina had said how she'd been chatting with people all day in the shade.

One of the young worship leaders from church, Jesse, brought a drum Andy didn't know what it was called, but was tribal in appearance with its long shape and rawhide top. It looked heavy.

He jerked his head at it. "That will get heavy. Are you sure you want to take it?"

Jesse looped the strap over his tall, lanky frame. "It's fine. I think it will be a good way to finish." He drummed out an awesome rhythm.

Andy noticed immediately the shift in the walkers. Although his step wasn't springy, the others had picked up their pace. Like soldiers and warriors over the centuries whose morale boosted when the band played. From his own Scottish heritage, the bagpipes were classified as an 'instrument of war' because of the lift in morale it gave the Scots, and in terrifying their opponents.

He nodded. "Thanks, Jesse. It really means a lot."

The little band marched up Manly beach for the last time to the sounds of drums and singing. Dad's voice was one of the loudest.

Full dark had settled by the time they made their way on the return path.

Someone had brought torches to light the way across the uneven terrain. Andy tried to step in the footprints, but with so many people walking with him, it was impossible. The drum kept up a constant beat, and they found their steps matching it.

It had been a long and difficult day. The mental and emotional toll almost had him weaving his steps as they made it back to the packed-up marquees. He took a deep breath and exhaled. He couldn't have done any of this without his supporters.

The drum stopped and the silence took over.

Nobody spoke as he headed one slow step at a time up onto the boardwalk and towards the memorial for fallen soldiers further down the open mall.

The weary bunch followed along behind him. It had been a long day for all, but there was one final thing he wanted to do.

Since returning from the war, he hadn't laid a wreath at a memorial. He played his bagpipers for others to lay them instead on ANZAC Day and Remembrance Day. This was his first opportunity to say thank you for the ultimate price paid by the fallen, so others experience freedom.

Each face from the photos he'd stared at all day as he walked past. Every father, brother, son.

He cradled the flower wreath in his hands and with shaky arms and legs, he bent down to one knee on the hard cobblestones. He laid it against the memorial, and hoisted back up to his feet. He wobbled, but then straightened.

In the silence, Andy drew his arm up to salute his gratitude, and honour their ultimate sacrifice.

He would not forget.

11

September, 2014

Tina slowly got out of bed so she didn't disturb Andy. Stealthy. She was a ninja sneaking out of her bedroom towards the boys' room. Callum was talking to Lachie.

"Good morning, my darlings."

Lachie sat up and stretched, his arms reaching for the roof. "Wow, Lachie, have you grown? Your arms are so long now." He'd turned eight and was due a growth spurt.

"Did I grow, Mummy?" Five-year old Callum's voice piped up from the bottom bunk.

"I don't know, sweetheart, did you?" She bent over to peek in his bed. A smile played around her mouth at his cuteness. "We'll have to check later. Right now, I have a special job for you both."

Lachie groaned and Callum jumped on the bed.

"Callum, stop jumping." She leaned in close to them and fake-whispered, "It's Father's Day today!"

Callum jumped again excitedly and Lachie smiled his gentle grin.

"Callum! I said, 'stop jumping'." He kept going. "Callum." At her serious tone he finally stilled, peering up at her with a guilty gleam in his innocent eyes. She'd give him ten seconds before he couldn't help himself. She needed to get him away from temptation. "Come on," she said, turning her back and holding her arms out. "Let's have a horsey-ride."

Lachie carefully climbed down the ladder. "What's the special job? Do we need to write on Daddy's card?"

"Yep." Callum leaped onto her back. "Ugh." She hoisted him into a more comfortable position. "Come on, it's in the guest bedroom."

She closed the guest room door after them. The bed was covered in bags and random items from when she'd 'cleaned up' last. The twinge of guilt ballooned and her shoulders slumped. It didn't matter how hard she tried, she couldn't seem to keep on top of the housework. She pushed the items towards the pillow end and grabbed the bags of gifts.

It was so hard buying presents for Andy. What did you get someone who never seemed to want anything? She handed Lachie the card and a pen. "Here, sweetheart, you write on the card on this side. Callum?" She made sure to get his attention from the treasures surrounding him. "Can you write your name and draw a picture for Daddy on this page, please?"

He nodded. "Yep." He reached out a chubby hand.

"When Lachie's finished, you can have a turn, okay?"

"'kay."

"What about you, Mummy?" Lachie asked.

"I've got a card to write on, too." She waved hers. "But first I need to wrap the presents." She rifled through the bags. "Oh, boys, here's the ones you got from the Father's Day stall at school. Do you want to wrap it, or do you want me to wrap it?"

"You wrap it." They chorused.

"Alright." She pulled out a mug that spoke to her when she bought it. *'Behind every great kid is a great Dad'* was written on both sides. She smiled. Their boys were going to look back on their life and be thankful for the great dad that Andy was. That was her hope.

Sure, he didn't engage with the boys, and he often only spoke to them harshly. She did everything for their sons, except to put them to bed at night. Lately, though, they'd been asking for her to tuck them in, but she resisted. It was Andy's only time he connected with them.

They finished their preparations. "Come on, you two." She collected everything and headed for the door. "Let's go wake Daddy."

———

ANDY HEARD THEM COMING. TINA WASN'T QUIET IN THE mornings. The boys' giggles drew nearer until they landed on him, and the breath rushed out of his chest.

"Happy Father's Day." Their voices blended and mashed together.

"Thanks, boys," he croaked.

Tina sat on the side of the bed. Two presents, one from each set of little hands, were thrust in his face. He didn't deserve presents, but he made the effort for his boys. He rubbed his face, his hand catching on the stubble. Shuffling up the bed and propping up on pillows, he took the presents still hanging near his face. The cards were eye-roll worthy, making jokes of him being like a monkey. Whoever coined the term 'dad-joke' didn't know his wife. "Did you choose this?" He asked her, shaking his head at the terrible joke.

She grinned and her face lit up. "Nope. The boys chose that." She laid a hand on her chest and gushed. "I'm so proud."

He didn't hold back the eye roll this time.

She deflated. "Actually, they just liked the monkeys." She rolled her eyes back at him.

"Did you read what I wrote?" Lachie asked in his quiet voice.

Callum bounced on the bed. "Did you read what I wrote?" He parroted.

"Not yet." Andy twisted his head to understand the scrawl. "Did you write this, Lachie?"

He beamed back at him. "Yep. Mum helped me with the spelling."

"You did a good job." He turned his attention to his other son, pointing at the squiggles and lettering on the opposite page. "I like your picture, Callum—"

"They're words," Tina interrupted. "Callum wrote on your card too, but since it's hard for us to read it, Callum's going to read it to you." She nodded at Callum to go ahead.

"To Daddy, Happy Father's Day. I love you to the moon and back. Love, Callum." Callum pointed his finger along the scribbles that circled the page as he 'read' the words. All Andy processed was 'To Daddy' and 'Callum'. "You did a good job, Callum, thank you." He wished this was over. He didn't deserve it.

He opened the first present. An alarm clock. Father's Day stalls were mostly junk, but the light on Lachie's face made it worthwhile. "Thanks, Lachie."

"Did you choose this by yourself?" Tina asked.

"Yep."

She cocked her head with a cheeky smile playing around her lips. "What made you choose a clock?" The smile turned mischievous. "Does Daddy need an alarm clock?"

"Yeah, 'cause he always sleeps in late."

The nightmares made sure of it.

The smile wiped off her face. "That's cause Daddy needs lots of sleep." Andy didn't think the boys would hear the false brightness in her tone. Yet another reminder that he sucked as a father. "Callum," she said, motioning towards him. "Do you want to give Daddy your gift?"

The present was shoved into his face again. It was too early for this. He jerked his head back and took the present. A mug. "Behind every great kid is a great dad," he read aloud. That wasn't true. He was a terrible father. He barely spent time with the kids, and he had no patience for them or their mess. Loving them and wanting to give them more than he currently was, just increased the guilt. Each day was getting harder. The battle to survive took more and more out of him. He had nothing left to give anybody. If they were great kids it was because of Tina, not because of him. "Ah, thanks Callum." Nothing like a gift that reminded you of everything you weren't.

"Here, this is the main present." She handed it to him. "Happy Father's Day."

He opened the last one, a bottle of his favourite whisky. Gifts he could do without, but whisky was always welcome. It wasn't a coping strategy anymore, but a nip that he looked forward to sometimes at the end of long days. Today looked like it was going to be one of those days.

THE HEADLINES WERE THE SAME, BUT STILL ANDY TUNED IN. He liked to stay in touch with what was happening in the world. He had to be ready to face whatever came their way.

Tina put the ebook reader down and sighed. "I suppose I better get the boys their dinner."

Andy turned up the TV. She always talked when he was trying to watch the afternoon news. She hated the news and refused to watch it; he preferred to know what was going on in the world.

The words of the newsreader chilled him to the core. Young Caucasian men were travelling to the Middle East to join the terrorist groups. He rubbed his bald head backwards and forwards. Young men in Australia. Joining terrorists. The words ricocheted around in his mind on an endless loop. The ad break shocked him out of his silence. "Did you hear that?" He turned to Tina to gauge her response, his heart cold with fear.

"Yeah. That's terrible."

Terrible? Didn't she get it? "Young Aussies are going to fight with the Taliban. Why would they do that?"

"I guess they get brainwashed online."

"But they're not even Middle Eastern." The words blurted out.

"Not all terrorists are of Middle Eastern descent." She stood up and walked towards the kitchen.

He thought of the IRA and other terrorists groups. He knew not all terrorists were Middle Eastern, but it hadn't really hit him until now. He followed her. "That means that anyone could be a terrorist."

She shrugged. "Well, yeah, I guess. Potentially. They're just young kids, targeted online. Hopefully, they'll realise their mistake and come home."

He stilled at the thought of them coming back into the country. "The government won't let them back in. Not easily." A tremor shook down his spine. But what about ones who don't leave the country? What if they did something here?

November, 2014

FEAR KNOTTED IN ANDY'S GUT. HE KNEW WHAT TINA WAS GOING to say before the words left her mouth.

"You have to go, honey," she said, as she cut up the meat for dinner. "I know it's in Sydney and you don't like being around lots of people, but it's your friend's fiftieth. You have to go. What would Alice tell you?"

She had him there. Andy exhaled a frustrated breath.

Alice made him confront the things he was avoiding. He stared at his feet. He didn't want to go to Sydney for a reason. He'd been avoiding his family and friends. They didn't know he had PTSD. He'd tried explaining to Tina why he hadn't told them, but he wasn't sure she understood. There was something about admitting to them that he couldn't cope with everyday life. Who wanted to admit to people they'd looked up to for so long that they were failing at living?

"And honey," she continued, "I understand you don't want your family and friends to think less of you, but you'll need to communicate to them what's going on with you. If you have to leave suddenly, they need to know why."

He didn't want to agree. "I know." He blew out his breath. "I'll give Les a call tonight."

After dinner, he headed into the bedroom to make the call while Tina put the boys to bed.

One of Les' daughters answered the phone, and he chatted for a little about what they were up to. "Hey, Anne, is your dad home?" She called out and then he heard Les' voice on other end. "Hey Les, how're going?"

They chatted before he got to the reason for the call.

"Listen, Les, we'll be at your birthday party, but I need to tell you something about what's going on with me." He took a deep breath before continuing, "I've been diagnosed with Post Traumatic Stress Disorder from my time in the Middle East."

"What does that mean?" Les' compassionate voice invited him to open up.

He explained about the Ramp Ceremonies, his part in them and how it affected him. Everything from nightmares and flashbacks to his struggles being around large groups of people. Especially with those young kids joining the terrorists. It made him uneasy. Visiting Sydney would be difficult since the restaurant they were going to, was in the heart of the Middle Eastern Sydney community.

Les listened patiently before asking, "Is there anything that we can do for you? Is it best that you don't come? I mean, I want you to come, but if it's too hard for you…"

"No, Alice, my psych, would never let me get away with it. I'm not allowed to avoid situations that cause me discomfort. If I have to leave suddenly, I want you to understand why." He fidgeted with a hair tie he found on the tall boy, winding it around his fingers until it grew painful. He could only imagine what his mate thought of him now.

They moved onto other subjects, and it grew easier to breathe. He asked after Les' wife, Kasey, and their three girls. Les asked after Tina and the boys. They said goodbye and Andy entered the lounge room where Tina was already sitting with her book.

She looked up. "How did it go?" She put the book down and moved towards him, studying his face. He wasn't sure what she saw, but she came in for a hug. "I'm so proud of you."

His breath caught in his chest. "That was really hard."

She pulled back. "I know. But at least now if something happens, Les will understand. Your relationship with him is important, and this clears up any potential for misunderstandings."

He cleared away the sudden frog in his throat and held the back of his head. "Admitting to my friend that I have PTSD was hard. I've always looked up to him and I feel like I've let him down."

"What? How can you have let him down?"

"I dunno." He shrugged. "It's just how I feel."

They sat in their respective places on the couch and settled in for another night, but his mind wasn't on the TV. Instead, his mind played pictures of what might happen in the heart of Sydney.

12

Andy became snippier the closer they drove to Sydney. Tina looked out the passenger window to not react to his sudden shift in mood. They'd hit the outskirts and Andy had gone from quiet to increasingly anxious. Although the traffic normally drove him nuts, this time his tone had an extra edge as he accused the drivers around him. The desire the snap at him welled up until she squashed it. It would only make things worse. *Think of what Andy's going through.*

She glanced over, his left leg was shifting and bouncing.

He ran a hand through his non-existent hair, massaging his scalp. "I hate Sydney drivers."

Time to distract. "It's funny how you get used to other cities. I bet you didn't think anything of it when you were younger."

"Yeah," he said, flicking his gaze to her. "But the amount of people on the roads now is just insane. It never used to be this bad."

Going through the traffic to get to the restaurant seemed to take forever, or maybe it just felt that way with the tension in the car.

"Are we there yet?" Callum piped up from the backseat. The boys were still munching on their McDonalds from the M1 stop. There was no way they'd eat Thai food.

"Not yet." Hopefully soon.

"We're about five minutes away. I'll park at a parking area Les was telling me about and we'll walk over to the restaurant from there."

Andy pointed it out as they drove past.

"What are you doing? Didn't you just say that we're parking there?" She couldn't keep the alarm from her voice. Surely he hadn't changed his mind.

He snapped, "I know where I'm going." Sweat beaded on his forehead. "I just want to scope out the area first."

Tina inhaled deeply to keep her words to herself. He was highly stressed, she reminded herself. She exhaled. "Okay."

He circled their Ford Territory back to the car park and pulled into a spot. Tina moved to unbuckle her seat belt, but Andy's hand shot out, stilling her. "What's wrong?"

"Just—I just need a minute." He studied the surrounding people.

She settled back into the seat. "Okay." Puzzled by this new behaviour she asked, "Are you okay?"

He continued to scan their surroundings, brow furrowed in a fierce glare.

"Why aren't we getting out the car?" Lachie asked.

Ugh. How would she explain his father was looking for terrorists? "Because."

"Because why?"

Heart pinging, she turned around in her seat. *God, give me the words.*

"Well, Lachie, you know how Daddy went away to war?" He nodded. "Something happened to his brain, his mind, because of it. All of the thinking got mixed up so now he sees danger everywhere." She shot Andy a look to see if he was okay with her description, but he was too focused on their surroundings.

"Daddy needs our patience and our help. Do you think you can be patient with him and help him if he needs it?"

Lachie puffed out his chest. "Yep."

Tina smiled. "That's awesome. We'll go to the restaurant when Daddy's ready."

Andy nodded. "Just wait in the car for a minute. I want to check and make sure…" He stopped speaking when he glanced in the back. But she knew what he meant, make sure they were safe from an attack.

He got out the car and scanned the area, focusing in particular on the people on the opposite side of the road. Their clothing gave away their Middle Eastern heritage. He leaned down and spoke into the car. "It's fine."

They got out and Andy pointed them in the direction they needed to go. They passed people and shops on the way. Andy scowled at everyone. She pushed the embarrassment aside. It was difficult for him to be around so many people he didn't know or trust.

They turned into a small street wide enough for a single car. Although it was fairly crowded being a Saturday evening, it flowed easily in both directions.

Tina struggled to watch where she was going and monitor Callum. He hated holding hands, often walking in front of the group so he didn't have to. His tendency to run off and follow whatever caught his eye had her on edge. With so many people around, he could easily get lost.

Suddenly aware that Andy wasn't walking next to her anymore, she turned and glanced behind, puzzled.

Andy had stopped walking and was hunched over as if trying to curl up into himself. His hand reached for his head. What the heck? She turned back the few steps and reached out her hand.

THE RAMP CEREMONY HAD APPEARED OUT OF NOWHERE. ANDY blinked. The soldiers on either side of him remained formed up. His bagpipes were under his arm and the weight of the drones leaned on his left shoulder.

He took a deep breath, the smell of aircraft fuel invading his nostrils as he filled the bag. The sweet notes of the tune echoed around them. He slow marched behind the caskets draped in the Canadian flag—

Something touched his arm, the flashback disappeared. Unfamiliar sights and sounds assaulted his senses.

Looking up, he dropped his hand. Tina's mouth moved.

A deep humiliation filled him. Had he been slow marching up the street, pretending to play the bagpipes?

People parted around them like they were rocks in a river bed, their confused expressions deepening his worry and fear he'd made an idiot of himself.

"Are you okay?"

He focused on Tina's words. Her expression of love and compassion had him confessing. "I had a flashback."

He wiped clammy hands on his trousers.

Her shoulders slumped slightly before she straightened up again. "Okay," she said, looping her arm through his. She looked around as if around searching. "Callum! Callum!" As usual, Callum ignored her call.

Lachie turned to his brother. "Callum! Stop."

They were beginning to draw more attention to themselves.

Andy felt her tug on his arm. "You're okay. We can get through this. Let's just get to the restaurant."

He nodded, his tight throat robbing him of speech.

Callum had stopped so Lachie turned back to them. "What's wrong with Daddy?"

Shame danced on his downtrodden soul.

"Daddy's brain just got a bit confused, sweetheart. Remember how I said we can help him?"

Lachie took steps towards him and held out his hand. "I can help you, Daddy."

Andy fought back tears that threatened to turn him into a greater mess. He cleared his throat. "Thanks, Lachie." He clasped onto the little hand and tried not to hold it too tightly.

Tina nodded approvingly and released his arm. "Callum, I know you don't like holding hands, but there's too many people." She grabbed his hand and ploughed through the crowd as if they didn't even exist.

He wished he could do the same. All eyes seemed stuck on him.

Within a few minutes they arrived at the Thai restaurant. As much as he wanted to take a minute before walking in, Tina had already opened the door and started down the narrow walkway to the function rooms at the back of the restaurant.

The narrow corridor blurred and morphed into the fuselage of the Orion aircraft. The warning sirens were blaring and lights were flashing. A missile was hot on their tail.

"Go! Go! Go!"

He was running almost in place, the plane's sudden turn meant running towards the back where the parachutes were kept was impossible—

"Honey?" Tina was walking back towards him and he almost crumpled at her feet.

He met her concerned blue eyes. "I just had another flashback."

Her mouth fell open.

He didn't remember getting to the function room, but as soon as he saw Les, he fell into his arms.

TINA STRUGGLED TO HOLD HERSELF TOGETHER WATCHING ANDY crumple into his oldest friend's arms. She furiously blinked away her tears.

Les silently asked her what was wrong.

"He just had two flashbacks. One the way here, and then just now coming up the corridor to the function room."

Les nodded and patted Andy's back. "You're safe. I've got you."

Les's wife, Kasey, came over. Shock and alarm covered her features. "Is Andy alright?"

Tina hugged her tightly. "Not really. It's the PTSD. But he's here. I'm not sure if you've got seating organised, but Andy will need to sit with his back to the wall and close to the exit." She scanned the room and gestured to the opposite side of the room. "Do you mind if we sit over at this end?"

"I figured the kids could sit over there together so the adults could talk at the other end of the room." Kasey waved her hand towards the rest of the adults were sitting.

"We don't mind sitting with the kids. In fact, it would probably be a good idea to take his mind off the flashbacks."

Kasey rubbed Tina's arm. "Of course, if that's what he needs."

Tina walked over as the friends pulled away from each other. "Happy birthday, Les." She hugged him briefly before resting her arm around Andy's back. She motioned with her head. "We can sit over on that side of the room. You can have the seat on the end, so your back is to the wall and you're close to the exit if you need to leave."

"Thanks," he croaked out, relief and gratitude collapsing his shoulders.

Her lips tugged up in a half-smile. Andy needed to feel safe in his environment, and he could do that best if he could watch everything that happened.

THE DISCUSSIONS WENT ON AROUND HIM. THE YOUNG ADULTS, THE teenagers and kids down to their boys as the youngest. Some of Kasey's family were there as well to help them celebrate, so the room was full of people.

He tried not to think about it.

He pulled out his handkerchief and mopped his wet brow. Movement in the corridor caught his attention. An Asian male, the server, entered with the plates of entrees. He studied his apron. Could a bomb fit under there? The server left and Andy's mind eased slightly.

Another server entered. He called out an order and one of his nieces responded. The server headed towards them. Andy's muscles flexed as he prepared to launch at the slightest hint of violence. The young man balanced his arm load, leaning in close to the group and putting the plate down. Andy couldn't take it anymore and snapped, "Just leave it on the table. We'll sort it out."

Tina looped her arm through his tense one. "Honey, it's okay. He's just doing his job."

Doesn't mean he trusted him though.

He scowled at the server.

The sudden silence caught his attention.

Cassie, Addy, Anne, and their cousins on Kasey's side of the family stared at him in shock.

The server met his gaze, put the plates down and left.

Tina filled the awkward silence. "This is why we're sitting here. I don't know if your dad told you, but Andy has Post Traumatic Stress Disorder from his time in the Middle East. He doesn't feel safe in Sydney, so being here this evening is huge for him." She squeezed his arm, but he couldn't look up. He didn't want to see the looks on the girls' faces. She continued to his shame, "He had a couple of flashbacks on the way over and his anxiety levels are probably fairly high right now."

It took everything in him not to grab his family and run out of there.

He sneaked a peek at the girls' expressions. They looked like rabbits caught in the headlights of a car.

Tina drew in a breath. "But, he's here." She squeezed his arm again. "And we get to spend time with all you girls." She added. "How's the nursing course going at Uni?"

Andy tuned out the conversation and turned to Lachie and Callum sitting further down the table with cousins more their own age. Callum was trying a spring roll, but Lachie turned his nose up at everything. No surprise, it was why they'd gotten Drive-Thru on the way.

Voices floated around him, but he wasn't participating in any of the conversations. He couldn't concentrate.

Before long, the servers came back to take the dirty plates. Talk around the main meal had his heart pounding. There was no way he could handle more servers coming in and out of the room with each course.

He reached down and grasped his leg to stop it jiggling.

His breathing shallowed and he blinked rapidly to focus.

"It's time to go," he said, picking up Tina's bag from under the table. "Come on, boys. It's time to go."

He stood up, not waiting for his family and went over to Les. "I'm sorry, mate, but I need to go. Happy birthday."

Les stood up and threw an arm around his shoulders. "I'll walk out with you. Where's your car?"

"We parked about two minutes away. You don't have to come out with us."

Les shook his head, determined. "Nope. I'm walking you out."

"But it's your birthday." He didn't want to spoil the evening.

"Yep, that means I get to decide what I want, and this is what I want."

Andy looked over his shoulder at Tina, who'd grabbed her handbag off him and was saying their farewells to the rest of the guests.

Andy turned, left the room and froze.

Les plowed into his back, but he braced his hand on the wall.

"What's wrong?" Les asked him.

His voice trembled, "I don't want to have another flashback."

"I've got you, mate." Les placed his large hand on his back.

As a family, they all surrounded him and started moving up the corridor. One side of the wall opened up to another section of the restaurant and he felt the stares of the diners as they passed. Did they see him have the flashback earlier? What had he done? Run in place?

Les looped his arm over his shoulder again when they made it outside. "Which way?"

"I have no idea." Tina piped up.

He pointed in the direction they'd come. They walked down the side street only wide enough for a single car. There were fewer people now than before.

They came to a gap. He flung out his arm, jerking Les to a stop. "Wait."

They piled up behind up as he stuck his head around the corner. Nothing. "Okay, we can move."

At the next opening, he pulled them up short again, but when he stuck his head around the corner there was too much blocking his vision. It would be the perfect spot for an ambush. He kept his hand out blocking them from moving.

"Is everything okay?" Les asked.

Andy collapsed against the rough bricks. "I can't—I can't—." He tried to suck in oxygen. He shook his head, words failing him as the fear strangled him.

Les looked between him and Tina as if he couldn't believe what he was witnessing. Andy brought his hand up to his head. Still sucking in huge breaths. "There could be anyone there." He managed to gasp out. "Someone could ambush us."

"Come on," Les said, as he pulled Andy tight to his chest. "I've got you. I'll keep you safe."

Andy tucked his head down.

"What's wrong, Mummy?" Lachie asked. *Your father is having a mental breakdown.* "Will Daddy be okay?"

"Yeah, Daddy will be fine, sweetheart. We'll look after him, and Les is helping Daddy."

They made it past the intersection, but Les didn't let go of him as they continued down the sloped road. At least the car was at the bottom of the hill.

The car.

He pulled up short. "I need you all to stay here."

"What? Why?" Tina asked.

He dragged her away from the boys. "I need to check for a bomb."

Understanding and compassion filled her blue eyes, and she nodded. She turned to the boys. "We're going to stay over here while Daddy checks to make sure the car is ready to go. Okay, boys?" Her bright tone made it sound like he wasn't losing his mind.

"Is he normally like this?" Les asked her as Andy walked towards the car.

He heard Tina's reply before he got out of earshot. "No, it's never been this bad before."

He scanned the surroundings before approaching the vehicle. No one was in sight. He performed a visual check around it. He got to his hands and knees, the small stones biting into his flesh as he peered underneath. All clear.

He pulled the car keys out of his pocket and flicked his gaze to his family before pressing the unlock button. Nothing. He released a breath, but jerked in another as he grasped hold of the door handle. The door cracked open. He flinched. Nothing happened.

He sat in the driver's seat, his hands trembling as he put the keys in the ignition. Maybe this was it. He turned the key, only half expecting to survive it. The engine caught. He sagged into the seat. His galloping heart rate slowed. He moved his sluggish body out of the car and called, "It's fine, you can come over now."

Tina and Les brought the boys the remaining thirty metres and the two boys climbed into their car seats. Tina buckled them in while Andy faced his mate.

Les drew him in for another hug and with tears sliding down his cheeks, he confessed, "I had no idea." Les pulled back. "I knew you were raising awareness with the 40 for 40, but I didn't know you were suffering."

Andy cleared his throat. "I didn't want you to know." It still shamed him that his oldest friend had to help him to the car, but it was also a relief to not hide it anymore.

Tina hugged Les goodbye. "Thank you. For your support. It helps."

The way back towards Newcastle was silent, Tina lost in another book and the boys asleep in the back. Andy took a deep breath, the tight band constricting his chest easing the closer he got to home.

Within days, any semblance of peace shattered.

13

Andy walked into the lunchroom a few days later. The guys were close to the TV, which was on full volume. The breaking news story set an icy fear through his veins.

There was a terrorist attack in Sydney.

His mind blanked and then raced as he caught the location. Martin Place. That was where Les worked.

His phone was out of his pocket and he was dialling his friend before he registered his actions.

"I'm alright, Andy." Les's voice reassured him a little.

"Where are you?"

"I'm at work."

Andy cursed, that was only two blocks from the cafe where the terrorists were holed up.

Les continued, "But I'm fine. I'm safe."

Nowhere was safe. Especially in Sydney.

The TV caught his attention again. "Les." Worry and panic spiked his voice. "You need to get out of there."

"We've been told to stay in the offices."

"The media are saying they've got bombs." Les had to get out of there. He had to leave. Who cared what they were told to do?

There. Were. Bombs.

Hysteria amplified his voice. "You've got to go. You can't stay. Police are doing a search of all the buildings for more bombs. They've got the dogs checking."

"Okay." Les voice was still calm. Why wasn't he freaking out? "I'll get out of here."

He released a little of the tension gripping him. "Okay." His mind raced with options. "Take your car and just leave the city. Go home. No! Don't go home." He thought of all the Middle Eastern families that lived near Les. "Go to your Mum and Dad's."

"Okay, I'm going." Andy heard sounds like movement in the background. "I've got to go and check on the others."

"No!" He yelled through the phone. "You need to get out of there."

"Andy, I'm a manager, I have to make sure that my people are being looked after."

It was a reasonable argument, but he wasn't happy. "Okay. I understand. But you leave," he insisted.

"I will."

"Call me when you get to your parents."

"Okay. Bye."

"Bye, I love ya, mate."

"Love you, too," Les replied, just before he hung up the phone.

Andy stared at his mobile phone and wondered if he'd ever see his friend again.

THE FAMILY PILED OUT OF THE CAR. TINA STRUGGLED TO KEEP HER temper in. Andy had been in a foul mood all morning. What was his problem?

The irony didn't escape her notice that her annoyance with him on their way to church was in opposition to the place all about love and peace.

Definitely not feeling loving or peaceful, she thought, darkly.

Andy dragged his heels crossing the car park.

"What's wrong?" She asked, trying to temper the snark in her tone.

"I don't feel safe."

Tina frowned in confusion, pausing on the third stair and turning to face him. "But we've been here plenty of times before. You know these people."

He stopped at the bottom of the steps but refused look up at her. "It's the new people that concern me."

"How do you know there will be new people?"

"There were last week."

Huh. She hadn't noticed. Embarrassment pinked her cheeks. "Oh. Why is that a problem?"

"The siege in Sydney. Terrorists could be anyone, anywhere."

Understanding suddenly enveloped her. The siege during the week had affected his thoughts. Before, the war was 'over there', now it had been brought home. She grew sad, realising he didn't feel safe in his own country anymore.

How could she make this work for him?

"What if we sat at the back of the church, next to the exit, instead of at the front? Would that help you?" Andy could leave quickly and easily if he needed to.

He met her eyes for the first time all morning. "Yeah," he replied, nodding as if psyching himself up to climb the steps.

They received a few strange looks from people when they realised that they weren't in their usual spot. Tina returned a bland smile. Andy wouldn't want them to make a fuss.

At morning tea, she searched for him after she'd caught up with several people. She scanned the few people left before checking the alfresco. Nope. She ducked back into the church auditorium.

Lachie and Callum were running laps around the room with some other kids while Andy had tucked himself away in a corner.

Fortunately, he wasn't alone. Brian sat with him. Her soul eased, seeing he was okay.

"Boys! You want to run around, run around outside!" Tina called out to them all.

They took off for the nearest exit.

"Sorry, Chris," Tina said as she approached the Pastor.

Chris waved her hand. "They were fine. There isn't really anyone left in here to run into."

Chris picked up one of the chairs to begin stacking them along the wall. "How are you going, Tina?" The genuineness of the question warmed her heart.

"Not great, actually, Chris. Andy's not doing too well at the moment." Tina reached for one end of a group of chairs.

Chris grabbed the other end and they took it to the stack. "I noticed you guys weren't in your usual seats."

"Andy hasn't responded well to the attack in Sydney. He nearly didn't make it inside today. But we sat at the back on purpose, cause that's where he feels safest. Against the wall, there isn't anyone behind him." She motioned to where they'd sat as she went to the next group of chairs. "The last couple of weeks I noticed he's been turning around in his chair scowling at people. I realised this morning it's because his back is vulnerable and he doesn't trust new people."

"If sitting at the back is what he needs to do to feel safe..." Chris' voice trailed off and she laughed a little. "Shakes the congregation up when people sit in different seats," she said with a cheeky smile before asking compassionately, "Is there anything that we can do for you both?"

Tina shook her head. "Besides keeping us in your prayers, not really. Andy's going back to Alice, his psychologist."

"Had he stopped seeing her?"

"No, he hadn't stopped, but he was down to three-monthly visits before all this happened. He called her this week past, and he's now back on weekly visits." Tina sighed and added, "He's been looking for roadside bombs on his way to work every day."

Chris' eyebrows shot up before glancing towards Andy in compassion. "Why is he looking for roadside bombs? He didn't do that in the war, did he?"

"The fears aren't rational. We're not sure where it comes from. Alice's puzzled by it as well, and wants to investigate with him more. She's seen it before, but with the Army guys she works with. Andy deployed with the Air Force, not with the Army. We're all confused why he's behaving like that."

Andy came over and helped with some of the chairs, picking up a set by himself and stacking it.

"Show off," she teased him. The words escaping from her before she remembered he'd lost his sense of humour.

He stared back at her.

February, 2015

ANOTHER WALK. TINA SIGHED. *REALLY, GOD? ANOTHER ONE?* SHE focused back on Andy's words as he spelt out his plan to walk from Newcastle to the Lindt cafe in Martin Place, Sydney. The scene that had triggered his downward spiral.

Andy sat forward on the couch and asked, "Can you pray about it?" He fidgeted with one of her hair bands. Winding it around and around his fingers before releasing it and starting again. Just like these damn walks. Winding him up, causing pain and then doing it all over again.

She closed her eyes and her soul roared unspoken words. The walk on Manly Beach had taken so much out of him, and out of them as a family. The long hours of training taking so much from him physically, there was nothing left for the family. His PTSD symptoms had lessened, but he still couldn't engage with them.

Now his symptoms were the worst they'd ever been and he wanted to add another walk to it.

She breathed out the silent arguments and surrendered to what God wanted. *Lord? Do You want Andy to do this walk?*

Yes.

Why? She railed at Him like a toddler having a tantrum. *Haven't we been through enough? Why do we have to add more? You know how much the last walk took out of Andy—out of all of us.* Visions of Andy breaking down in front of the photos on Manly Beach filled her mind's eye. *I can't handle Andy putting himself through that misery again.*

It won't be like that. It will be a walk of victory and celebration.

Fine. She couldn't help the childish tone.

Opening her eyes, she met his waiting gaze. "I believe God wants you to do the walk."

"Are you sure?" Instead of reassuring him, her words seemed to cause him worry.

"Yep." She popped the 'p'. "I know it's Him, because I don't want you to do it."

He leaned back, warily. "Why don't you want me to do it?"

She shrugged a shoulder. "The last walk was so painful for you. I don't want you to go through that again, and I don't want to watch you suffer."

"Dad said that watching me walk on Manly Beach was one of the hardest things he'd had to do as a parent. To watch me suffer and not be able to do anything about it."

It was the hardest thing to do as a wife as well. "How do you plan on doing this?" She leaned over and cupped her mug of tea, testing its temperature.

He laid out his idea of walking around 40kms each day—without added weight, she'd made sure—for four days, until he reached the last checkpoint. "On the last morning, I'll wait at the bottom of the Harbour Bridge, there's a grassed area. If you and the boys could meet me there, I thought we could walk across the bridge together and into the city. I might take a while because I'll need to psych myself up for it. I'll probably have a panic attack."

'It will be a walk of victory and celebration' came back to her mind, and she saw in her mind's eye, Andy happy, peaceful and excited to move forward. Her brow furrowed as she concentrated on the image. "I think it's going to be easy for you. God said the walk was going to be a walk of victory and celebration. At least, that's what I believe."

He glanced at her as if she was crazy. "I'm doing this walk because I'm terrified of going to Sydney. I need to face my fears." His voice broke.

She strove for comforting words. "I don't know how and I don't know why, but I believe this walk is going to be a walk of freedom, not of fear." He shook his head. He didn't believe her, and that was okay. But she had to hold onto that hope. It was the only way she could handle the months of training ahead. A thought slammed into her. "When do you want to do it?"

"In the winter. It's too hot to try and walk in the warmer months."

"Next year?"

"No, this year. Next year's too far away."

"That's only six months away," she blurted.

"I know."

"But the training—"

He raised a hand to stop her. "I haven't lost that much fitness since the Manly walk. I'll need to build up my stamina, though. I'll have to do longer distances and back-to-back training days."

She trusted him to work it out, but she inwardly slumped at the extra cost on her family. "You know we'll support you." Her lips turned up in a smile. "Whatever you need, we're behind you."

March, 2015

THE SILENCE OF THE EMPTY HOUSE SPLINTERED AS TINA SLAMMED the front door.

She breathed through the emotional pain, her hands

clenching into fists. Her parents invited them over to have dinner along with her brother and his wife. Mum and Dad been living in the area for a couple of months and she'd barely seen them. Andy had one pitiful excuse after another why they couldn't go and visit. Can't afford the extra petrol money. Can't go for dinner, it's too much on the boys. She hated that all the excuses meant none of them could go. The fury she'd held back from him reared its head. How dare he? Nothing was more important to her than her loved ones and he was making her choose between him and her parents.

She threw her bag down in the corner of their room and paced the width of the bed, imagining all the things she'd say to him. But when he stood in her mind's eye, she saw the suffering on his face and remembered it wasn't his fault. The fury seemed to roar at her, but she held it back again. *PTSD* was the reason he didn't socialise. The reason he didn't even go to the shops anymore. Why he was avoiding everything in life except work. PTSD was harder to visualise, but she flowed her rage toward it anyway. The release left her hollow and empty. She slumped down on the bedcovers.

Andy had been doing so well. And then the siege triggered some switch inside him and he'd regressed so far backwards he'd become almost unrecognisable.

The hollow feeling widened until it became a gaping maw inside. The promises of God felt just as empty. He'd promised her, deep in her spirit Andy would come through it. Friends and strangers had told her that they believed God said to them He would heal Andy.

But what if God didn't?

Was this going to be the rest of their lives?

A voice she hadn't heard in a long time interjected, *divorce him.*

No. They'd promised each other in sickness and in health. This was sickness. Just one they couldn't see. Divorce wasn't an option for her. She refused to make it one.

She thought of the years ahead and cried. *I can't do this. It's so hard. I don't want to live the rest of our lives like this.* Her chest shuddered on an inhale. *But if that's what happens, I trust You, Lord. I hate the idea of it, but if You choose not to heal Andy, I will still love You and follow You.*

She curled up into a ball on her bed, closed her eyes and tried to draw into the space where she felt her loving Heavenly Father.

You need to learn to lean on others, My Darling Girl.

But why? I only need You.

It is not good for 'man' to be alone. Love infused the words, warming her and filling the emptiness.

Tina's heart broke anew, feeling rejected and not at the same time. It was the first time that God had refused to directly comfort her. She'd normally 'feel' His arms wrap around her. But this time He wanted to use someone else's arms to hug her.

Tina withdrew deep inside herself. She didn't want to be that vulnerable. Who would understand? It had to be someone that wouldn't judge Andy, that would continue to love him, in spite of anything that she shared.

Helen.

Yes. Helen. She would understand. Brian's health struggles meant that Helen was more than a wife, she was also a carer.

So am I.

The epiphany rocked her soul.

She grabbed her mobile phone from her bag and typed a message to Helen.

TINA: I REALLY NEED YOU. CAN YOU PLEASE COME OVER?

HELEN: I'LL BE THERE IN A FEW MINUTES.

. . .

WHEN HELEN ARRIVED, THE TEARS BEGAN AGAIN AND THEY DIDN'T stop. Years worth of struggle and pain poured out in words and sobs while Helen cradled her in motherly arms and gently stroked her hair. The empathy from one who had been there before her brought more than peace and comfort.

It was the realisation she wasn't alone.

14

T ina smiled at her friends as they found a seat in the busy
coffee shop. During the last couple of years, she'd made
some close relationships at the church. Friends who were more
like family. Women who loved her and accepted her as she was,
and she did the same for them.

But still she found it difficult to share how she was feeling.
Since her breakdown with Helen, she'd started learning how to
let others into her emotional state.

It had been past time to tell her best friends about how she
was coping with Andy's PTSD.

"How did you feel when you found out about Andy's suicide
attempt?" Tina's best friend sat around a table a busy cafe. A rare
chance the three of them had to hang out together. Zowie asked
the question Tina had struggled to answer herself.

"I was shocked, I guess. You know how you go numb
sometimes?"

"How long ago did it happen?" Tash asked.

Tina paused, setting her mug back down. "When I found out,
it was over a year before. It made the attempt a little harder to

process in some ways. On one hand, he's alive and I'm relieved and grateful. While on the other hand, I think I could've lost him. I'd be a widow with two young children. I'm jobless. We live in Defence Housing, so I would have lost the house and moved back in with my parents. All while mourning him and not understanding why. He said he didn't write a note." She teared up. "One of the boys would probably have found him."

"That sucks." She loved how Zowie said it like it was.

"Yeah. It could've been so bad."

Tash cut off the corner of her cheesecake. "Amazing the psychologist 'just happened' to be at the church."

Tina nodded. "I still get goose bumps. We found out recently through Alice, Captain Felix usually travelled north inland, but that time he went via the coast." She shook her head, still disbelieving all the pieces that went into saving her husband's life. "And of all of the churches in the area he could have gone to, he came to ours. To me, it's too much coincidence to be anything but God."

Zowie started a story about one of her kids as Tina ate the last of her gooey caramel slice and leaned back in her chair. They discussed their kid problems and bandied about ideas to help each other.

"I hate you have to go through this as a single mum." Tina commented when Tash disclosed her own problems. "Andy's not contributing in the way of parenting, but at least he's there." By the grace of God.

"What do you mean?" Zowie tucked her hair behind her ear.

She shrugged a shoulder to mask her hurt. "Andy's mentally checked out. He's in survival mode. His goal for each day is simply to get to the next one, so there's nothing left to give to me or the kids."

"Sounds lonely."

Yep. She shrugged again. "I cope. It's one reason I read so much. My way of escaping from reality." She laughed. "And why my house is always a mess."

Tash's eyes crinkled as she laughed as well. "I love that about you. It makes me feel better about my place."

Tina laughed, but the loneliness of her marriage echoed deep.

"HOW DID IT GO WITH ALICE?" TINA ASKED ANDY LATER THAT week as he finished telling her about work.

He smiled. He'd been waiting for the opportunity to tell her. "She thinks she knows what's caused the 'switch to flip'." Excitement seeped into his tone. "She asked me when I look for roadside bombs on the way to work if it was like I'm on patrol." Something that he'd done in his infantry days. He put his coffee cup on the small table next to his spot on the couch.

"Of course. That makes sense." Tina nodded.

"Alice then asked if I'd been through debriefing—"

"What's that?"

He scowled at her interruption. "I'm getting to that. Anyway, I didn't understand what she was talking about, so she explained it's like the old-school "de-programming'. Because I was in a combat role in the infantry, I was supposed to get debriefed before I switched over to the RAAF."

"Did you get debriefed? I don't remember."

"After my transfer paperwork was accepted for the Air Force, I spent a week in 'holding'. Alice said I should have seen the psychs then." He shook his head. "But I didn't. Someone thought since I was transferring to the Air Force it wasn't necessary."

"So what's Alice going to do?" She asked.

"We'll go through the debriefing, and I have homework to do."

Tina winced. He understood, the exposure therapy had sucked.

His lips quirked wryly. "I don't have to do exposure therapy, but I'm not allowed to avoid things anymore."

Her blue eyes held his. "Ah."

He shifted in his seat. "Alice said I need to go to the shops for you. It's my homework because, I don't know if you realise it, but I'd been avoiding going." He dropped his gaze.

Tina half-laughed. "I know you've been avoiding the shops. You've been avoiding everything where there's people."

He jerked his head up. She'd known?

"Especially," she continued, "family. Mine and yours." Her eyes pinned him.

He swallowed a lump in his throat. He didn't realise she'd picked up on that.

Tina smiled at him. "But I understand."

He couldn't meet her eyes.

He knew he'd hurt her every time he'd said they couldn't see their family. Petrol money. Don't have time, too busy. He'd used any and every excuse to avoid them all. He flicked his gaze up. "I'm sorry."

Tina came over and he shifted to make room for her. "Honey, I know this isn't you. It's the PTSD. This is not who you are."

"But don't you ever get angry with me?" He tried not to show how much her response would impact him. Hurting his family just about killed him.

"Sometimes, but I eventually remember that I'm angry at PTSD. Not you. It changed the way your brain processes information. Going to see Alice is helping you to re-write those thought patterns."

"How do you know that?" Alice had told him today that's what they would do with the anxiety he had in large groups of people.

"I've been doing some research about PTSD online. Did you know that they use to believe that the adult brain couldn't be 're-wired'? But recent studies have proven that the brain is capable of change. They call it neuroplasticity."

His chest burned with love for her. She'd taken the time to research more about PTSD. "Alice told me about it today."

She continued, "How can I be angry with you? You didn't choose to have PTSD. It happened to you." Her eyes turned fierce. "I get really, really angry with PTSD, but not with you." She shook her head. "It's not your fault."

He was humbled by her unbelievable words. It still felt like his fault. The breakdown in relationships, his over-reactions, the overwhelming hatred he still felt towards Muslims.

"When are you going to do your homework?"

Her question caught him off-guard. He shrugged a shoulder. "Do you need anything from the shops?"

Tina grinned at him. "Actually, yes. I was waiting for you to get home before I left so I didn't have to take Callum and Lachie with me."

Apprehension tingled up his spine. "How much do you need? Alice said to get a few items to start with."

"It's about five things." She sighed. "I was looking forward to getting out the house for a bit…" She shrugged. "That's okay, though. If you have homework I'd rather you do that."

His stomach churned, the coffee souring. "When do you need me to go?"

"There's nothing urgent on the list. How about if you go after the boys are in bed. Woolies is practically empty from about 8 o'clock."

Relief only half eased the turmoil. It was a good idea.

He tried not to dwell on the shopping trip for the next couple of hours, but the more he thought about it, the more he stressed.

He drummed his fingers on his leg and checked the clock. It was time.

Andy checked for roadside bombs on the way. Scanned the area for threats like he'd been trained.

He pulled into the car park and sat in the car for a minute, scouting the open area. Eventually, he got out and stood outside the front doors, trying to calm himself.

He had Alice's voice in his ear telling him to breathe and bring his anxiety level down. *Who was that?* An older man caught his attention.

The doors opened. He wasn't ready.

He rocked back and forth a few times before walking into the foyer. Next to the trolleys were the hand baskets.

What was that person doing? The clear glass doors gave him an unrestricted view of the front check-outs. Another person went to the next aisle.

He looked at the green plastic stacked in front of him. How did he get one from the pile?

His heart pounded like he was running his fitness assessment.

Time seemed to stretch on for an eternity as he looked down at baskets.

Another shopper appeared in his periphery.

Was he a threat? Another person. *What's in her purse?*

He needed to get this done as quickly as possible. This wasn't a safe place to be. He reached for the black handles and snatched a basket off the top. His arm looped through the handles. He could use this.

A shield.

A weapon.

He patted the plastic with his other hand, testing it. Not ideal, but it would work.

The short shopping list crumpled in his hand and he tried to smooth the list open as he entered the supermarket.

The fruit and veg section was empty of people. One person behind the deli counter. A manager and checkout person by the registers. He kept his eye on them and tried to read the list at the same time.

Bacon.

That meant the deli.

He cautiously approached the middle-aged woman behind the counter. *Who is she? What's she got under that apron?* A bomb would fit under there.

His steps slowed as he got closer. He stared her down.

She gave him a strange look. "Can I help you?"

He continued to scrutinise her.

"Sir? Can I get you anything?"

He flicked his gaze down briefly to the small goods display. "Bacon. I need bacon."

"How much would you like?"

"Umm…" He looked at the shopping list. It didn't say.

"150g? 250?" She asked.

"250g."

Her gloved hand dived into the bacon and she pulled out a handful. It weighed over two-fifty on the scales. He didn't care. She opened her mouth to speak, but something in his expression must have had her re-think the wisdom of that.

She wrapped the bacon and returned, handing over the paper-covered parcel. "Can I get you anything else?"

He stared at her, shook his head and slowly reached out to take the package.

Backing up a few steps, he continued to stare her down before turning to the side and to the first aisle. He checked the list. Four more items. *When was this torture going to end?*

He scanned the store before heading towards the baking aisle. His heart thumped in his head when he approached the middle section. *What's under the shelves? Someone could be hiding under there.*

Andy bent down to peer under the closest shelf. No bomb. No person. It would take him a while to search under each shelf without a mirror to aid him. A shopper walked past the end of the aisle. His head swivelled from side to side trying to watch both ends at the same time.

It was the perfect spot for an ambush.

He had nowhere to go.

Andy snatched the flour from the shelf and scanned the items on the list as he ran towards the end of the aisle.

I have to get out of here.

He sprinted from aisle to aisle, barely paying attention to what he needed to get before slowing to a jog as he approached the registers. The self-serve was still open.

Thank God.

He put the shopping through the machine and impatiently waited with his card ready. As soon as the display changed, he tapped his card on the EFTPOS machine, ripping the receipt out as it cut and hightailed it to the exit.

As soon as the fresh air greeted him, his body began to shake.

He reached in his pocket for the keys and pulled them out. He walked to the car only a few paces from the door.

What did the keys do? How do I get in the car? And get home.

His legs collapsed from under him, and he sat in the gutter. Cradling his head in his trembling hands, his chest heaved with sobs.

He couldn't remember how to get in his car.

How long he sat there, he didn't know. The ache in his chest eventually eased, but his throat felt raw. The weight of the keys were heavy in his hand. What did he do with them? There were buttons on them. What would happen if he pushed one?

The locks on the car disengaged and the internal light shone in the darkness. His shoulders collapsed in relief and he opened the door.

He needed to get home. To safety.

He shoved the key in a small hole and turned it. The engine started. His mind went on autopilot and his body operated the vehicle without his assistance.

Ignoring speed limits, he made the two-minute trip in one and pulled up the steep driveway.

He bolted out the car, shopping bag swinging with momentum, and he opened the front door.

"Where have you bee—" Tina started to ask.

Home.

Safety.

He fell into her arms and cried.

TINA'S HEART HAD ACHED FOR HER HUSBAND AS SHE LISTENED TO him describe what he'd been thinking at the supermarket. Her eyes had welled up as Andy detailed sitting in the gutter unable to get in the car and back home to safety.

She rolled over in bed, unable to get to sleep.

God, what kind of life is this?

Silence answered with nothing.

She flopped onto her back.

I thought You were going to heal Andy. I believed You promised in that bible verse that he would get through this. But it's worse now.

What if God didn't heal Andy now, in this life. She had faith in healing, but sometimes that didn't come until heaven - the place without pain and suffering. Would God make them wait this long? The years stretched out before her.

Could she really do this for the next few decades?

The bleak despair that came with that thought threatened. The hope of a better future for their family dulled in its wake.

Where is your hope anchored?

The gentle voice of her Lord brought light spearing through the darkness of the despair. Her hope was in her God, not in the circumstances of her life. If He chose not to heal Andy until the end of his life, then He would give her the strength that she needed.

Was it selfish of her to wish that He would heal Andy now? This was not the life she wanted to have.

April, 2015

TINA SMILED TO HERSELF AS SHE STARED AT THE SCENERY PASSING on their way to the hobby shop. This time, she'd make it work. The idea for Andy to do a hobby had occurred to her last week. When he wasn't at work, he sat in front of the TV and dwelled.

She wanted to get him out of his head and thinking about something else.

She'd asked him, "You used to make models when you were a kid, didn't you?"

"Yeah, model planes."

"Have you thought about starting that again?"

A light had shone in his eyes, as if the idea gave him something positive to hold onto.

Andy had already decided which model he was going to do when he browsed the online shop. He'd chosen to build a wooden sailing ship instead of a plane. Alice had thought it was an excellent idea, even more so because he would have to go to the shop in person.

It had become his homework task. Andy wasn't allowed to leave the shop until his anxiety levels had reduced down to a five out of ten. Tina didn't want another supermarket incident, so she'd asked him if he wanted her to come.

This time she would support him the entire time.

Andy's anxiety showed itself in his impatience with other drivers the closer they got to the shop. In the terse way he spoke to her and the boys. In the way he snapped at her when they got out the car.

"Boys, I want you to stay with Mum and me. Callum, no running off."

"They'll be fine. The shop is just up there." She pointed a couple hundred metres behind them.

"They still have to cross the road, and it's a busy road." He snapped, "I'm just trying to keep them safe."

Ah. This was about their safety, and not only road safety. She internally battled the stubborn desire to snap back at him. "Come on boys, hold hands while we cross. It is a busy road."

On the other side, Tina let go of Callum's hand and took hold of Andy's. It was cool to touch and slightly clammy. She fought the urge to wipe her hands and gripped his tighter.

He gripped hers back.

She smiled. "Come on. You can do this."

Andy hesitated as the automatic doors opened but together, they walked up the slight ramp into the shop. Products lined every available space.

Lachie had paused in the entrance, his jaw hanging open at the model trains in front of him. Trains had been his passion since he was old enough to hold one. "Lachie, Callum." She made sure she had eye contact. "I need you to stay with me." She reached out and grabbed Callum before he took off into the depths of the shop. "We'll get the model ship that Daddy wants to build, and then we'll come back and explore all this stuff. Okay?"

They agreed, and together they followed Andy as he powered through the shop, following the signs to the correct area. Within minutes, he located the ship he wanted to build, tucked the box under his arm and prepared to head off to the checkout.

"Let's go." He was obviously mission focused.

What? He was leaving already?

Wait a minute. She narrowed her eyes. He was trying to leave as quickly as possible, but that wasn't the homework.

She raised an eyebrow. "I think we should look around the shop for a little bit first."

Guilt flashed across his features. Busted.

His shoulders slumped. "Fine."

Tina wandered with Lachie and Callum around the model ship section looking at all the different kinds for ten minutes before saying, "Let's go to the counter."

Andy beelined for the front of the shop and waited behind the person currently being served. He sighed. Shifted his weight. Shifted again. "Come on already, it doesn't take all day." He murmured louder than was polite.

She caught his arm in warning. "Honey."

"What?" He glanced at her in consternation.

Before she could say anything the customer left and Andy stepped up to the counter.

"Good morning, how are you today?" The middle-aged sales person asked.

"Good, thanks," They both replied the standard greeting.

"Is this all today?"

"Yeah—"

"Is everything that's needed to build the ship in the box?" She asked at the same time as Andy tried to get out of the shop fast.

The man looked puzzled. "Yeah, everything is in the box for the ship. You won't need to buy any more pieces."

Tina shook her head. "No, I mean, is there any equipment that we need to buy to build the ship, or is everything that he needs already in the box?" She jerked her thumb in Andy's direction.

The sales man looked from her to Andy and back again. "Ah, you'll need tools."

"I'm sorry, I haven't explained myself very well. My husband hasn't done one of these before and wants to build this. He has nothing. Can you tell us what tools, then, he'll need to make it?"

Still giving Andy strange looks, he showed them to a nearby wall covered in hardware of all different shapes and sizes. It was overwhelming looking at it.

She noticed in her periphery Andy shooting glances at the people around them, looking stressed.

The man pointed out the different gadgets that Andy would need, drawing him into the conversation, but seeing he didn't have his full attention, the sales man turned to speak to Tina. "If you like, I can just show you what he needs to get started?"

Andy interjected, his patience obviously vanished, "Yeah, that would be great. Listen, I have Post Traumatic Stress Disorder from the war in Iraq and Afghanistan. It's really hard for me to be here right now." He peeked over his shoulder. "I'm in here because my psychologist thought doing a model would help me get my mind off what's going on in my head. Just tell me what I need to get started and then I'll get some other stuff along the way."

The sales man took a step back, but nodded his head

respectfully. "Sure." He grabbed five items from the shelves. "These should get you started." He took them back over to the counter and rang up the purchases.

Andy drummed his fingers while Tina paid for it all.

She looked around for Lachie and Callum. They were both transfixed by the model trains running behind the glass. They were fine.

Andy was not.

He grabbed the plastic bag and turned to leave the shop.

Tina caught his arm again. "What's your anxiety levels out of ten?"

He rolled his lips inward and lowered his head. "Ten."

Not time to go yet.

She tilted her head and pulled him over to where the boys were. "How about we have a look around before we go? What did Alice say to do to get your levels down?"

He scowled. "She said to use my grounding techniques."

She remembered what those were, so she commented and pointed up at the display going above their heads. "Did you see the plane up there? How cool is that? It's got bright colours."

He focused on where she was pointing but stayed silent.

What else? "How many trains are going around the track? I can see… one… two, three… four…"

"Five, six," Lachie piped up.

"Good spotting, Lachie."

"Is that a barn? What's the train doing over there?" She prattled on for the next five minutes and as each minute passed, the tension in Andy's biceps faded. "How's your levels now?"

"About a seven."

She nodded and dragged Andy towards the aisles. "Let's see the LEGO aisle."

He didn't look happy with her, but he followed.

It was hard commenting on all the things she saw. Noticing the fine details wasn't hard, but speaking out everything she noticed was wearing a little thin. "What about you boys, what things can you see?"

They took over pointing out different objects, the things they would like to buy. Lachie's eyes shone like he was in a cave filled with treasure.

Andy's arm was almost relaxed under her hand. "How's your levels now?"

He thought about it. "Five." *Thank God.*

She grinned. "I'm proud of you, she said, jerking her head towards the exit. "Now, we can go."

15

Andy drummed his fingers while he waited for Tina to return to the lounge room after putting the boys to bed.

He'd had something come to him while he was training for the walk from Newcastle to Sydney. It terrified him. But the idea kept coming, almost nagging at him, so he wanted to ask Tina what she thought about it.

He sat up a little straighter as she entered the room and sat on her favourite recliner.

"What are you watching?" She asked, as she reached for her ebook reader on the side table.

"I dunno. Nothin'." He couldn't focus on anything. But he flicked through some channels anyway to see what else was on. Maybe he'd find something to distract him.

Tina focused on her book and he knew he'd lost her, and his chance.

He sighed and turned his full attention to the TV. Re-runs of one of his favourite comedic sitcoms came on and he tried to turn off his brain.

Andy tapped his leg with his fingertips.

Her voice broke through his concentration. "Are you alright, over there?"

He jerked his head her way.

What was she talking about? "Huh?"

She motioned to his hands. "You're fidgeting. Is something wrong?"

He was both waiting for this moment and hoping it would never come. He launched into it. "I have something that I'd like you to pray about and see what you think…" His voice trailed off, not wanting to finish the sentence.

"Yeah, okay…?"

The words tumbled out of his mouth, "I think God wants me to go to a Mosque."

"What?" She started in surprise. "What for?" Genuine curiosity infused her tone.

"I think He wants me to talk to the Imam and ask for forgiveness for the hatred I had towards muslims."

THE SHOCK FELL AWAY FROM TINA AS SHE FOCUSED ON THOSE words. Mosque. Hatred. Forgiveness. A warmth filled her and she knew the source was from outside herself. A sense of 'right' and certainty came with it.

"I believe this is what God wants too."

"I think I'm supposed to go in uniform."

Trepidation momentarily eclipsed the warmth as she replied, "Perhaps you should ask Pastor Chris and maybe some others you trust to hear from God. It's an enormous thing. You'll want to make sure it's what He wants." *Especially if you're going in your military uniform.*

Andy nodded. "That's why I was asking you, but I think asking Chris as well is a good idea."

The following Sunday, Andy approached several people at church he trusted and it was unanimous. All believed and agreed this was something that God wanted. Chris had suggested asking a member of the church who used to be a Pastor in Sydney and had formed relationships with Muslims there. He'd suggested a particular Mosque in Sydney to speak to.

At home later that day, Tina typed in the name of it into her search engine and the Mosque's beautiful building appeared on the screen. The thought of calling or emailing the Mosque had caused Andy's naturally olive-like complexion to whiten so she'd offered to contact them for him.

She clicked on the Contact Us tab and set about writing an email, asking for Andy to make an appointment with the Imam. She wrote what he wanted to do; to ask forgiveness for the hatred he'd had towards Muslims, including how he wanted to come in his military uniform.

Saying a silent prayer, she clicked send.

THE WAVES CRASHED OVER THE SAND AND A SENSE OF PEACE FILLED Andy. It was too cool to go in the water, but walking on the wet sand was one of Andy and Tina's favourite ways to spend a Date Day. With both boys in school this year, the rare time Andy had time off work during school hours were golden opportunities. Even if the July winter wind had a bite.

The seagulls harassed them over lunch, their cries shrill as they begged for the tasty fish and chips.

Andy pulled up his sleeve and checked the time. They'd better head off. "We'll need to go, so we can be back in time to pick up the boys from school."

Tina nodded, but she still had a faraway expression.

"Tina?"

She looked at him this time. "I heard you, I'm just not ready yet to go back. I love the sound of waves." She inhaled deeply. "And the salty breeze." It played about her hair, twisting and turning it into a tangled mess. She tucked it behind her ear as he pressed the unlock button on the car's remote.

He had just done up his seatbelt when Tina's phone rang.

"Your phone is ringing," he said, when she didn't make a move to answer it.

"Oh!" She fumbled with her bag, arm disappearing into its depths before she pulled it out and answered it just before it rang out.

Andy rolled his eyes and shook his head. She never answered her phone. It drove him nuts.

"Yes, this is her." Tina listened for a moment before stabbing him with alarmed eyes.

Fierce protectiveness had him scowling at whoever was on the other end of the phone. Was it the boys? Had something happened to them at school? Maybe he should start the car. He turned the ignition, ready to get moving as soon as she said where to go. Who *was* on the other end?

She must have read the question on his face because she held her hand over the microphone and leaned towards him. "It's the Mosque."

He cursed. His hand fell away from the keys and he sat back in his seat, ears tuned to every word.

"Oh— yes, that's right. Andy would like to come to the Mosque." A long pause. "Yes, will that be a problem? It's something that he feels he needs to do. We understand that coming in uniform might raise a few issues, but Andy doesn't intend any harm. He only wants to speak to the Imam and ask forgiveness for the how he felt towards Muslims because of his time in the war."

Ribbons of anxiety weaved together in his gut.

What if they said no?

What if they said yes?

He turned off the engine.

"Tonight?" Tina practically yelped the word, her voice echoing in the sudden silence.

Tonight? Air rushed out of his lungs. *That wasn't enough time.* He wasn't prepared.

"Can I get back to you?" Another pause. "The number came up on the screen, so if I call you back on this number, will that be alright?" She bobbed her head up and down. "Okay, great. Thanks for getting back to us, and I'll give you a call back in a few minutes." Another pause. Her blue eyes held his. "No, it's just that we're in Newcastle at the moment and if Andy's going to be there for 7pm, then he'll need to decide soon." She raised her eyebrows at him before saying, "I'll let you know shortly, thanks again. Bye."

Words failed him.

"They want to know if you can come to the Mosque tonight at 7pm…"

His head shook no. "It's too short notice."

"Why?"

"I don't have time to get there."

"Yes, you do. How long will it take to get there?" She threw his argument back at him.

"About three hours, 'cause we'll get there at peak hour." *See? Sydney traffic.* It just wasn't feasible.

"What time would you have to leave to get there in time?"

No! She wasn't supposed to ask that. He frowned. "I'd have to leave at 4 o'clock at the latest. But I don't want to go alone." He cut the air with his hand. "And I won't take you and boys with me." *No way.* It wasn't safe.

Tina nodded at him like this is it. *But not now, not today. I can't do it.* The half-smile on his wife's compassionate face did him in. "I know we can't go. It'll be okay. I know this will be hard for you, but you can do it. God is with you. Remember, you felt that this is what He wants you to do. Brian said he would go with you, let's call him."

"And Jase. I want Jase there too," he blurted.

"Alright. I'll call Brian and you call Jase. What time do you need to leave?"

The mental calculations briefly distracted his racing mind. "Tell Brian I'll pick him up at half-past three."

A quick call later and both Brian and Jase were keen to join him. *Damn it.* He wished he could slow the whole thing down. It was like watching an impending train wreck.

"Shall I call them back and confirm?"

He didn't want her to. His silence must have said everything.

"Putting it off isn't going to make it easier. If you do it now, then you don't have time to work yourself up over it. Just get it done." She said it like it was the easiest thing in the world.

Sweat broke out on his brow and he absently wiped it away. "Okay. I'll go."

Four hours later, the lines of cars on the Motorway in front of Andy sent his anxiety higher. "We need to go back," he said to Brian and Jason. He gripped the steering wheel tighter and ran his hand over his shaved head. It trembled as he fisted the steering wheel again.

"No, it's okay." Brian and Jason both attempted to reassure him.

It wasn't okay. His enemies were all around. They could come from anywhere. *There are too many people, we're just a target.* A sitting duck in a line of ducks just waiting to be picked off.

Brian and Jase said something else, but the words dissipated. The roaring in his ears made it difficult to focus on the road in front of him. He didn't want to be there. Stuck in Sydney peak hour traffic going to a Mosque in Sydney. Was he insane? What if they tried to kill him? He was leading his friends into this war zone and they weren't prepared. *I don't want to do this.*

The rain poured down and Andy increased the speed of the windscreen wipers, the frantic pace making him even more jittery.

He fixed his eyes on a spot up ahead. An accident. That'd be right. It was a sign. He wasn't supposed to go. He'd get them all killed. Turning the car around was the logical choice.

Although he still had trouble hearing most of their words, he knew Brian and Jason were praying for him. The twisted knot in his chest eased slightly, and he drove past the opportunity to go back.

16

The Mosque dwarfed the skyline as Andy pulled into a car spot opposite. The doors were open on the building and the room was so full the crowd overflowed outside.

Anxiety twisted his insides. Acidic bile burned the back of his throat. He slammed his hand against his closed mouth. More sweat beaded on his cold and clammy skin.

Visions of him being decapitated flashed through his mind. Pushing them away left him trembling.

Brian and Jase reached for their doors and he forced himself to reach for his own. He leaned back inside the car to grab his military hat before straightening his uniform.

Muslim men were everywhere. What if they'd put a bomb on the car?

He dropped to his knees and searched under the car. A part of him knew he wouldn't find a bomb, but he had to make sure. It wasn't safe here. He wasn't safe.

Brian and Jase gave him strange looks but remained silent. He was grateful. Explaining the compulsion to search for a bomb was beyond him.

They made their way slowly across the road, Brian leaning heavily on his walking stick after being in the car for hours.

Andy's brain short-circuited.

He breathed deeply and stepped forward. The men turned around and fear as strong as what gripped him flared in their eyes.

"I'm here to speak to the Imam, can you please show me where I need to go?"

The men murmured. Was it Arabic? No one answered him in English.

The crowd parted as an older man in traditional Middle Eastern clothes stepped out of the crowd. "You are here to speak to the Imam, yes?"

"Yes, sir." Relief flared and extinguished, like a flame without enough fuel.

"Come this way." He held out his arm towards another building. Andy commanded his feet to follow. Brian and Jase trailed behind.

The man pushed open the doors into a large conference room and invited them to sit and wait. "The Imam will be with you shortly, he is finishing up prayers."

The three of them sat as the man left the room. Brian and Jase made idle talk, but Andy couldn't focus long enough on the conversation to join in.

He checked his watch for what felt like the hundredth time and sighed deeply. Then shifted in his seat. He played with the zipper on his pants leg, but stopped when his leg jiggled too much to continue.

What was taking so long? He checked the time again. Had it only been ten minutes?

The doors suddenly pushed inwards and the man from before entered with a man dressed in similarly, but with a large hat on his head. The Imam.

Introductions were made but Andy focused on the Imam, and what he planned to say. He'd learned the traditional Arabic greeting, but before he could get the words out, the Imam kept walking towards him with his arms held wide.

Shock paralysed Andy as the Imam's arms wrapped around him and patted his back before releasing him.

The traditional greeting fumbled off his tongue, "As-Salaam Ali...Ala...Alai—" He gave up trying to pronounce it, a little ashamed he'd failed since he'd been practicing. At least the Imam seemed to appreciate the effort.

After everyone found seats around the conference table, Andy began his story. "My name is Corporal Andrew Summers, my wife sent you an email to arrange this meeting." He continued, not withholding anything. He spoke of his time in the war. Of his friend who died. Of his suicide attempt and struggle with PTSD.

The Imam listened patiently, not taking his eyes off of him.

He lowered his gaze, but forced himself to make eye contact with the Imam again. "I hated Islam and Muslims in general." He thumped his chest with his fist. "But I am a follower of Jesus and it's tearing me apart because Jesus loves everyone." His voice grew thick in his throat. "I tarnished you all with the same brush as those who are destroying this world." He refused to dishonour his hosts by naming the group. "And I'm sorry. I'm asking if you have it in your heart to forgive me."

The air felt thick around him as he held his breath, waiting.

The Imam's mouth lifted in a smile. "I hugged you when I came in, didn't I? It is not hard to forgive someone who has been through as much as what you have. Islam is a peaceful faith. I can show you in the Qu'ran if you like? It is our holy text, like your bible."

Not sure, Andy looked over at Brian who nodded, smiling.

"Thank you, I'd like that."

The Imam brought the Qu'ran over and pointed out various passages that spoke of Islam as a peaceful and loving faith. "Like your bible, it needs to be read in context of the surrounding passages. You cannot just take a verse out of context."

Brian responded with something like agreement, but Andy was distracted.

Something was missing. Andy watched as the Imam flipped to another section of text as Andy mentally searched for what it was.

The answer hit like a punch to his abdomen.

He wasn't anxious.

At all.

When did that happen?

The Imam looked around. "Oh! We forgot the Turkish Delight!" He turned to his assistant who opened cupboards, pulling out a polished silver tray and serving Turkish Delight imported from the overseas.

"Would you like to view the Mosque?"

Making sure Brian and Jase were okay with it, Andy said, "Sure. That would be good."

They had a tour of the building, the Imam pointing out the different areas, what they were used for and why. It was really interesting and informative, hearing why women and men were segregated in worship. To honour women and to keep the worshipper's thoughts directed on Allah.

The small group turned around a corner of the building on their way back to the car. Two young muslim men came out of nowhere. Around their bodies were ribbons of a gold colour. Andy blinked, but it didn't disappear. He waved a polite hello as they passed and continued on to the car.

On the way home, Andy pulled into the McDonalds on the freeway between Sydney and Newcastle. All they'd had to eat was the delicious Turkish Delight.

Inside the restaurant, Andy stood in the long queue to order. Jason headed to the bathroom. When the food was ready, he pushed through the crowd to the table where Brian sat waiting. He put the tray down and sat, reaching for his meal in the same motion.

Andy was about to put his burger in his mouth when Brian asked, "Did you notice anything when you walked in?"

Huh? Did he notice anything. His confused expression must have said it all.

Brian repeated, "Did you notice anything when you walked in?" He motioned with his eyes around the room.

Andy looked around for the first time since he entered the restaurant. The McDonalds was full of young Middle Eastern men. From their clothing, they'd been to a soccer game and were on their way home.

His jaw slackened.

He was sitting in a room full of people that only a few hours earlier, he wouldn't have even entered.

He put his burger down and met Brian's eyes in wonder.

Brian smiled. "What do you see?"

He looked around again, and his vision shifted, focusing on the impossible. "I see gold. It's coming out of them."

These people are My creation.

He saw it, how God viewed the people group he had vilified in his mind. Their value stood out to him as if they were treasure.

Andy turned back to Brian. "He loves them so much. They have so much worth and value to Him." He was in awe.

Brian picked up his own burger and nodded. "That's right."

THE CAR ENGINE TURNED OFF AS TINA GLANCED AT THE CLOCK. IT was almost midnight. Her imagination had almost gotten the best of her, but she'd reined it back.

She met him at the door. The eyes of the husband she married stared back at her. Their eyes welled up. She opened her arms, and he embraced her.

She sobbed, "You're back. I can see it. Your eyes." She wasn't making sense. The man she'd fallen in love with was home.

"Something happened," he began, "I don't know how to explain it."

She pulled back and nodded. "I know. I can see it. I have my

Andy back." She pulled him close for a gentle peck. *Thank You, Lord!*

Andy went through to the kitchen and put the kettle on, telling her everything that happened from when they'd left to dinner at McDonalds.

"Wow."

He grinned. "I know."

"Wow."

Later, as she snuggled in her husband's arms, her mind raced with all that Andy had shared. The Lord had promised that Andy wouldn't suffer from PTSD forever, that He would heal him. Now that it had happened, it felt a little surreal. Her eyes drifted shut while her soul and spirit sang her to sleep with praises to her God.

August, 2015

It was Friday. Andy's tired legs ached from the four previous days walking from Newcastle to Sydney to raise awareness for PTSD. Four days without seeing his boys. Two days since he'd seen Tina.

His wife had walked with him every step of this journey through PTSD. The days were more often bad than good and a part of him still couldn't believe she'd stuck with him through it all.

Andy waited on the grassy hill where he'd planned to meet his family, friends and their support crew from Raymond Terrace Marketplace Management. This walk from Newcastle to Sydney had been tough. His feet—he didn't want to know what they looked like—were so painful. He'd spent about 40kms on them each day for four days and today he would cover the remaining ten.

He looked up at the Harbour Bridge in front of him and

remembered when he'd planned the walk. He'd expected to need this break to prepare himself to face his mental demon. Yet here he was, happy and excited to see his family. Thoughts of fear or anxiety didn't exist. His brain had rewired, but he didn't understand how. PTSD had dominated who he was and his way of life for eight years.

Now he was free.

His phone rang as he caught sight of them coming down the steep embankment, the boys racing down the hill towards him.

"Daddy! Daddy!" He bent down, arms open wide. First Lachie and then Callum almost bowled him over.

"Hey, boys. I missed you." They held on for a moment more and pushed away, racing and playing on the lush green grass.

He admired Tina as she carefully took steps on the slope. She'd taken the trip down to the Central Coast on Wednesday to spend an hour with him over lunch. He'd really struggled emotionally and mentally being away from his family.

"Hey, honey." Tina's arms slipped around his back. He leaned forward to kiss her.

Soon enough they were enclosed in a small group of family and friends that made the journey to support him.

Together, they walked over the bridge to George Street where the Sydney Seige had triggered the PTSD.

As he walked up the slight incline, Andy saw his father and more friends ahead. Tears stung his eyes and his throat ached. Seeing them here filled his heart with love.

He reached the cafe, feeling surreal. He placed a wreath against the wall of the cafe, stepped back and saluted.

It was closure. The end of a journey. He turned to his wife, their sons clinging to her side. As one they rushed forward to hug each other.

"I'm so proud of you." Tina's quiet words in his ear resounded within him. "You've come such a long way."

He squeezed her tighter until the boys complained and he released them.

"Where to now?" Tina asked.

That was the biggest question. What now? For so long his focus each day was survival. What would the future hold?

EPILOGUE

Wagga Wagga, NSW, Australia
September, 2017

Tina slowly got out of bed so she didn't disturb Andy. Stealthy. She was a ninja, sneaking out of her room towards the boys' room. They were lying in bed watching YouTube videos on their iPads.

"Good morning, my darlings," she said, walking close for their morning cuddle. They were growing up so fast. They'd recently had birthdays and the growth spurts that seemed to go with it. "Come on, let's go grab the presents."

Eleven year-old Lachie asked, "What presents?"

She laughed and shook her head. "Callum, do you remember who the presents are for?"

Callum threw back the covers and bounced up and down. She gave him a 'look' and he stopped. Eight years old and he still tried to jump on the bed.

"Daddy," Callum piped up.

Lachie climbed down the bunk and hugged her. "Oh, yeah."

"I remembered to send you to school with money for the

Father's Day Stall this year. Don't forget to get them out of their hiding spots," she warned them before continuing, "And make sure to write on Dad's card. I'll go and make his cup of tea."

Twenty minutes later the boys carried their presents through to the main bedroom. Tina grabbed the hot cup of tea on the way.

Callum jumped up on the bed. "Happy Father's Day, Daddy!"

"Happy Father's Day." Lachie said, much more quietly. She rubbed at his head, now reaching her shoulders.

Andy's eyes struggled to open. "Thanks, boys." His voice croaked. "What time is it?"

She grinned unashamedly. "Seven." Andy wasn't a morning person.

He groaned and rubbed his face, rolling onto his back.

"Here, Daddy." Callum thrust his present in Andy's face.

Within minutes, the bed was covered in gift wrap and envelopes. The boys left to get something to eat.

"Do you want some bacon and eggs?" Tina asked.

"Not yet. Give me time to wake up."

She'd finished making the boys pancakes when Andy came through the kitchen. "Are you ready for breakfast now?"

He sat on a stool at the breakfast bar and nodded, but seemed subdued.

"Is everything okay?"

Andy met her gaze. "Do you realise I've only been a father for two years?"

What the heck was he talking about? Lachie was eleven. "What do you mean, you've been a father for longer than that."

"I wasn't really a father when I had PTSD."

Oh. She gestured in his direction. "You—"

"I wasn't a father. Not really. You did everything. I've only been participating in their lives for two years."

Tina quieted. She couldn't argue with the facts. She let her hand fall. "That wasn't your fault."

"I know. You're so much better at parenting than me."

She snorted. "That's only because I've been doing it for longer. You'll get there. I'm not perfect, I make mistakes all the time." She stepped closer towards him until she reached the bench separating them. "You've come so far. It'll take time to develop a deeper relationship with the boys, but they love you already. That hasn't changed."

Andy's mouth lifted in a slight smile, but his face remained thoughtful.

———

August, 2018

"WHOSE TURN IS IT TO CHOOSE?" TINA CALLED OUT TO THE REST of the family as they prepared for family movie night.

"Mine!" Callum yelled.

"No, it was your turn last time." Lachie protested.

"No, it wasn't," Callum fired back.

"Yes, it was."

"Was not."

"Was too."

"Boys." Andy gave them both a 'look'. "Stop arguing. It was Mum's turn last time, so that means it's…." He pretended to think about it.

Callum bounced in front of him, hopefully.

Lachie's puppy dog eyes, pleaded.

He held their suspense for a little longer, a mischievous smile threatening to overtake his face. "Lachie," he began, "It's—"

"Yes!" Lachie fist pumped the air and 'flossed'.

"Not your turn."

Cries of "Yes!" and "Nooo!" deafened Andy. "What movie are you choosing, Callum?"

"Pokemon!"

Andy and Tina groaned in sync.

Tina turned to the kitchen. "Someone help me make popcorn?"

"Me!" Callum ran off to the pantry to get the kernels.

Tina brought a large bowl of buttered popcorn to the lounge room just as the movie was starting.

Andy grinned at her awed expression. He'd been just as surprised when the boys had argued over who was going to snuggle with him. He pulled them closer on each side.

Tina commented, "I see no-one wants to snuggle with me." She faked a sniffle.

The boys fell for it. They both moved to comfort her.

"I'll snuggle with you, Mum." Lachie couldn't bear to see Tina upset. It always broke his heart.

"Don't fall for it, Lachie." Andy warned, holding him back. "She's faking."

She pressed her hand to her chest. "Who me?" A wicked smile played on her lips. "Popcorn?"

November, 2018

"ON THREE — ONE, TWO, THREE." ANDY LIFTED HIS END OF THE kayak and together with Tina they took it down to the river. The boys followed behind chattering in excitement. Andy's aquatic shoes squelched in the mud, cooling his feet. After placing the red child-size kayak near the waters' edge they went back up to the trailer for the next one.

When all four kayaks were ready to go and lifesaver vests on, Andy helped his family onto the river. Droplets of icy-cold water fell on his sun-warmed skin and he rhythmically pulled himself along. They kept the boys to edges of the riverbank where the current wasn't as strong.

Andy looked over at his family, laughing and enjoying the river. They'd posted to a smaller rural community further inland and they loved the laid-back pace of life. Being separated from their support system had forced their little family to reconnect again.

Tina had made an offhand comment the night before that still lingered in his mind. They had flirted and teased each other right before she demanded a hug with tears in her eyes.

"I can't remember the last time you teased me," she'd said. It had brought tears to his own eyes. Light-hearted banter had been a hallmark of their relationship from the beginning. He hadn't noticed they'd stopped.

Now and then Tina opened up with what he'd been like to live with him during those years. The walking on eggshells. The efforts she took to help the boys understand what was happening to him, why he responded the way he did to them. Hardest of all was hearing her describe him as a jerk. The PTSD had changed him, and thank God he wasn't that person anymore.

After being medically cleared of PTSD since visiting the Mosque, his personal life focused on raising awareness for mental health issues, predominately PTSD in veterans and emergency services. He'd helped out several people in both careers over the years.

Andy sometimes spoke at conferences about his experiences and he invited Tina to speak with him. The attendees heard from him what brought him to the point of suicide, how if he'd received professional help earlier, he wouldn't have been in that position. From Tina they heard about what it was like living with someone with PTSD: caring for someone who lived to survive each day, who'd mentally and emotionally checked out of life.

Splashing and laughter tore him out of his reverie as Tina started a pirate fight.

It was a miracle. His recovery from PTSD and the unwavering love of his family.

"ARRRRRGGGHHH!" He yelled, bringing his kayak around with a gigantic spray of water, and he launched into the mock battle, a seasoned battler.

THE END...
And the beginning.

AFTERWORD

This story is by no means a comprehensive look at life with PTSD. For more information on Post Traumatic Stress Disorder, please visit any of the following websites:

Beyond Blue
    www.beyondblue.org.au

Black Dog Institute
    www.blackdoginstitute.org.au

Phoenix Australia
    www.phoenixaustralia.org

If you or a loved one is suffering from any mental health issues, please talk to a caring professional in your local area, or contact any of the above websites for help.

ACKNOWLEDGMENTS

Andrew and I would like to thank key people who have helped us on our journey, and in the development of this book.

Special thanks to Renee Conoulty for her encouragement and support in writing and publishing, and for Tamar Sloan for her time and effort in editing and providing feedback, any mistakes or errors are on us.

Thank you to the beta readers for their valuable feedback and comments.

A special mention to Jacinta Staines from The Trailblazer Society for her business coaching and advice that supported the final process. This might not have made it through the last stages without your wisdom, challenges and systems.

More thanks to our friends and family that have supported us over the years as we coped with the curveball life threw at us. There are too many to name, but you know who you are. You have our eternal gratitude.

Finally, to the One who decided this book was a good idea. Thank You, Lord, for Your faithfulness, strength, kindness and compassion when it all got too much. This is for You.

ABOUT THE AUTHORS

Tina Summers lives in Eastern Australia with her husband, Andrew, and two sons. She's both an author and an artist who enjoys creating new story-worlds and messing about with paint. If she's not in her office, studio or with family members, she's likely to be riding her motorbike to her favourite coffee shop.

Andrew Summers is a veteran of Afghanistan and Iraq. His openness and vulnerability in the struggles and journey through PTSD have inspired many to seek help for mental health issues. Andrew speaks at mental health conferences and forums, normalising conversations around mental health. He enjoys hikes, spending time with family and friends and riding his motorbike.